Early Modern Prayer

Special Issue of
*The Journal of Religious History,
Literature and Culture*
2017

Edited by
WILLIAM GIBSON
Oxford Brookes University

with

LAURA M. STEVENS
University of Tulsa

SABINE VOLK-BIRKE
Martin-Luther-Universität Halle-Wittenberg

Volume 3 November 2017 Number 2
UNIVERSITY OF WALES PRESS
https://doi.org/10.16922/jrhlc.3.2

Editors
Professor William Gibson, Oxford Brookes University
Dr John Morgan-Guy, University of Wales Trinity Saint David

Assistant Editor
Dr Thomas W. Smith, University of Leeds

Reviews Editor
Dr Nicky Tsougarakis, Edge Hill University

Editorial Advisory Board
Professor David Bebbington, Stirling University
Professor Stewart J. Brown, University of Edinburgh
Dr James J. Caudle, Yale University
Dr Robert G. Ingram, Ohio University, USA
Professor Geraint Jenkins, Aberystwyth University
Dr David Ceri Jones, Aberystwyth University
Professor J. Gwynfor Jones, Cardiff University
Dr Frances Knight, University of Nottingham
Professor Kenneth E. Roxburgh, Samford University, USA
Dr Robert Pope, University of Wales: Trinity Saint David
Professor Huw Pryce, Bangor University
Dr Eryn M. White, Aberystwyth University
Rt Revd and Rt Hon. Lord Williams of Oystermouth,
Magdalene College, Cambridge
Professor Jonathan Wooding, University of Sydney

Editorial Contacts
Professor William Gibson *wgibson@brookes.ac.uk*
Dr John Morgan-Guy *j.morgan-guy@uwtsd.ac.uk*
Dr Thomas W. Smith *T.W.Smith@leeds.ac.uk*
Dr Nicky Tsougarakis *tsougarn@edgehill.ac.uk*

Publishers and book reviewers with enquiries regarding reviews should contact the journal's reviews editor, Dr Nicky Tsougarakis *tsougarn@edgehill.ac.uk*

Cover illustration: Claude Mellan (attr.), frontispiece to the folio edition of François de Sales, *Introduction à la Vie Dévote* (1641) © The British Library Board.

CONTENTS

Contributors   v

Introduction: Early Modern Prayer
William Gibson, Laura M. Stevens and Sabine Volk-Birke   1

Rowlandson's 'Cover Story': The Revision of Private Devotional
Practice into Public Narrative
Denise M. Kohn   12

The Prayer of an Empress and the Death Penalty Moratorium
in Eighteenth-Century Russia
Elena Marasinova   36

The Captive at Prayer: Cross-Cultural Trauma as Revealed in
the Diary of Stephen Williams
Linda Meditz   56

The Eye of a Needle: Commemorating the 'Godly Merchant'
in the Early Modern Funeral Sermon
Penny Pritchard   70

Mary's Magnificat in Eighteenth-Century Britain and
New England
Laura M. Stevens   91

The Order and Methods of Nosegays: Mental Prayer in
François de Sales's *Introduction à la vie dévote* (1609) and its
Eighteenth-Century English Adaptations
Sabine Volk-Birke   108

Index   131

CONTRIBUTORS

William Gibson is Professor of Ecclesiastical History at Oxford Brookes University, UK.

Denise M. Kohn is Professor of English at Baldwin Wallace University, Ohio, USA.

Elena Marasinova is Chief of Research, Institute of Russian History, Russian Academy of Sciences and was a visiting professor at Columbia University, USA in 2015.

Linda Meditz received her PhD in History from the University of Connecticut in 2016.

Penny Pritchard is Senior Lecturer in English at Hertfordshire University, UK.

Laura M. Stevens is Associate Professor of English at the University of Tulsa, Oklahoma, USA.

Sabine Volk-Birke is Professor of English Studies at the Martin Luther University, Halle-Wittenberg, Germany.

INTRODUCTION: EARLY MODERN PRAYER

William Gibson, Laura M. Stevens and Sabine Volk-Birke

What was the place of prayer in the early modern world? What did it look and sound like? Of what aesthetic and political structures did it partake, and how did prayer affect art, literature and politics? How did the activities, expressions and texts we might group under the term prayer serve to bind disparate peoples together, or in turn to create friction and fissures within communities? What roles did prayer play in intercultural contact, including violence, conquest and resistance? How can we use the prayers of those centuries (roughly 1500–1800) imprecisely termed the 'early modern' era to understand the peoples, polities and cultures of that time?

Even if questions such as these are asked with a view to Christianity only, excluding other world religions, they impinge on the dynamics of transatlantic and intercultural relations, especially when Europeans engaged in intercontinental exploration, colonialism and conquest. Christopher Columbus initially denied that the populations he encountered in what he thought were the Indies participated in anything like prayer, having 'no religion of their own', thus supporting his assertion that these peoples 'could very easily become Christians'.[1] Amerigo Vespucci was similarly dismissive, noting in a letter describing his third voyage, 'here we were received with so many barbarous ceremonies that the pen will not suffice to write them down'.[2] Whether the peoples he encountered were engaged in rituals of hospitality or divine worship is unclear, but that Vespucci bypassed any consideration of the meaning of ceremonies says much about the dynamics of early intercontinental encounter. To recognize a foreign people's words or actions as prayer, if we consider prayer broadly to be attempted communication with what is transcendent, spiritual or divine, might be understood as an acknowledgement of some cultural substance and depth beyond what is dismissed out of hand as barbaric or primitive. A people without prayer is a people more easily, and with more ethical justification, transformed to suit one's own desires.

The determination of what counted as prayer and religious worship was at the centre of what has come to be known as the Chinese Rites Controversy, a dispute among Roman Catholic missionaries with very high stakes for the ascendancy of various religious orders within the Church but even more so for relations between the papacy and the Chinese emperor. Were Chinese rituals of honouring deceased ancestors, along with other imperial and Confucian ceremonies, essentially religious or civil? The answer to this question, hotly debated by Jesuit, Franciscan and Dominican missionaries in the seventeenth and eighteenth centuries, determined whether the Roman Catholic Church would demand that Chinese converts abandon these rituals, and indeed whether the Kangxi emperor would allow missionaries to continue to work in China.[3]

Recognizing prayer, and naming it as such, might be necessary to respectful intercultural communication, but it was far from sufficient. Hernan Cortés's awareness of an Aztec religion with a sophisticated set of rituals and prayers certainly did not prevent him from undertaking the conquest of the Aztec empire. Rather, it helped provide the visual language of conquest. Of Cortés's march on the capital city of Tenochtitlán, John Elliott noted, 'As they moved inland, they threw down "idols" and set up crosses in Indian places of worship.'[4] The colonization of New Spain, New England and New France is well known to have unfolded in part through the instruction of indigenous peoples in Christianity, but it was the adoption of these imported forms of prayer that often evidenced to Europeans the success of their missionary efforts. The more than a thousand Wampanoag, Narragansett, Massachusett, Nipmuc and other indigenous peoples who adopted the rigorous Reformed Christianity brought over by New England's Puritan colonists were known as 'Praying Indians'. This term figured prominently in promotional documents for the New England colonies, especially their missionary efforts, and it also played an important role in these converts' understanding and presentation of themselves.[5]

Colonial encounters had a transformative effect on both indigenous and imported modes of prayer. Much has been written about syncretism as a response to missionary activity, but there is a great deal more to be gained from studying prayer as a specific setting of word and action, both extempore and liturgical, in which cultures intersect with and alter each other. For example, Stephanie Schmidt's recent analysis of the *Cantares mexicanos*, an alphabetic Nahuatl-language manuscript from sixteenth-century Central Mexico, has found, amidst pre-Columbian songs, a song-dance connected with the gladiatorial rites of the Flaying of Men, in which war captives were ritually sacrificed, but in which Christian words and figures are present. '[N]am[ing] three sacred or exemplary figures – two Christian, one Mesoamerican – and locating each in a fundamental domain of the Nahua cosmos', this song-dance 'selectively accommodates elements of Christian thought but transmits an ethos of plurality in sacred matters'.[6] Patrick Erben has examined an entirely different situation two centuries later, in the English colony of Pennsylvania, in which Moravians originally from central Europe honed the practice of polyglot hymnody in collaboration with their Lenni Lenape and other converts, simultaneously singing the same hymn in several languages. Such an approach to prayer was designed to 'make possible "a mystical moment of Pentecostal unity of word and spirit"'. Through emigration, missionary activity and intercultural encounter, then, Moravians more fully realized their goal of 'achieving spiritual community' and developing 'a common spiritual language'.[7] Focusing on prayer as a fiercely contested yet supple medium of human expression can yield profound insights into the dynamics of contact and colonialism, especially for an era distinguished from preceding centuries most of all by dramatic increases in the scale and scope of intercultural encounter.

While missionary work in relation to non-Christian peoples highlights many issues connected with the forms and social practices of prayer more dramatically than interdenominational differences within Christianity, some of the prejudice, contempt and warfare seen in this context looks strikingly similar to the contests fought over prayer within Western societies. Although prayer could provide a basis for ecumenical understanding, it could also serve as the battleground for large and fierce controversies over the correct expression and form of belief and devotion.

Such vast questions of course cannot be tackled by a single journal issue. The publication of these six essays, however, highlights the need to identify an important field of study which still leaves much territory uncharted. It is also an attempt to outline some initial forays into this subject, with an admittedly narrow focus on examples of specifically Christian (if multi-denominational) prayer in Russia, France, Britain and New England. While some forms and forums of prayer have received attention from scholars in recent years, there has been little if any consideration of prayer as a subject that might productively be analysed across several regions and disciplines.

The areas in which prayer has impinged on scholarship are various and relate to a range of items, from texts to objects. Prayer spawned a range of material goods: prie-dieux, hassocks and kneelers, prayer cabinets, rosaries, portable altars and all manner of clothing for private devotions. Prayer was also performative; John Craig has examined the role of posture and gesture during prayers in churches.[8] Tara L. Lyons has suggested that in late Elizabethan theatre the use of prayer books as props was heavily symbolic, especially when used by women on the stage.[9] Prayer books formed one of the staples of the earliest publishing ventures; they were sure-fire sellers and remained so until the nineteenth century. The publication of books of prayer for private, domestic and communal use was common in the eighteenth century. One of these, *The New Week's Preparation for a worthy recipient of the Lord's Supper . . .*, was so popular that by 1775 it was in its thirty-sixth edition in Britain. One reason for its popularity was that the process of 'worthy preparation' for the Eucharist was recommended by the Church of England and encouraged by many clergy. In an era in which receipt of the Eucharist in England was growing from the canonical minimum of three times a year to monthly, and often weekly, such regular preparation was important to observe. The work was a series of prayers and meditations, including self-examination and confession of sins and a direction for the behaviour of the individual in the run-up to the Eucharist. Like many such works, it grew as accumulated elements were added by publishers. In the 1775 edition there were 'morning and evening prayer for the closet or family'.[10]

More recently the State Prayers Project in Britain has sought to collect together the various prayers issued by the Church on behalf of the state and assess them as a body.[11]

The project has shown that prayers could often be heavily political.[12] And specific prayers were written for ministers and politicians, suggesting that the separation of the religious and secular frames of mind had not happened quite as early as some have suggested.[13] Prayer was also sometimes seen as a source of satire and humour.[14]

Prayer was also the subject of controversy and denominational division. Issues such as the validity and purpose of extempore prayer as well as a settled liturgy were important debates in England this period.[15] The communal nature of prayer was clearly important in the eighteenth century and solidified ideas of society and communality.[16] Indeed, the identity of Anglicanism in the eighteenth century was certainly bound up with the use of the Book of Common Prayer, as it had been in earlier periods.[17] Beyond the established Church in England, prayer practice was divergent.[18] Between Protestants and Catholics the issue of the invocation of saints, prayers for the souls of the dead and prayers to the Virgin Mary were sources of fierce contention.[19] Some religious communities also developed distinctive prayer practices in the period.[20] So, despite the neglect of some aspects of prayer by scholars, it was an important aspect of early modern lives, and one which can have left few people untouched.

But what constituted prayer? The attempt to define it is fraught with controversy, then and now. Was prayer a 'conversation' with God, or an expression of piety and devotion that required no listening from Heaven? Were prayers expected to be answered, or were they the expressions of fallen and depraved humanity? The nature of prayer inevitably determined its form and function. The boundary between prayer and hymnody has been explored;[21] and the distinction between prayer and contemplation has also been considered.[22] Sometimes people observed and commented on different practices which were alien to their own.[23] Prayer could assume many forms: poetry, autobiography, collective prayer and also silence.[24] The degree to which private prayer could legitimately be held in a domestic setting has also been discussed.[25] Prayer has sometimes been treated as gendered and a preserve of, or reserved to, women.[26] Certainly, in some European contexts women were at the heart of religious devotion and prayer.[27] In some communities women were the means by which prayer was placed at the heart of domestic life.[28] The association of women with ecstatic and extreme forms of devotion was not uncommon in the early modern period, and prayer formed part of this gendering of religious observance.[29] These debates suggest that the nature of prayer was important to people in the early modern period, not just for their private religious lives, but also for their place in society.

These and other themes are examined in this collection of essays, most of which were contributions to a panel given at the International Congress for Eighteenth Century Studies at Rotterdam in 2015. The papers address the phenomenon of devotion in general and of prayer in particular, in the cultural, political and literary climate of the long eighteenth century, from a variety of perspectives and in a wide range of countries, while their findings intersect with a number of issues. If prayer was a particular form of expression within, and a means to achieve the fullness of, the spiritual life, then it was a familiar and habitual aspect of people's lives in this period. As such, it fulfilled a number of intellectual and emotional functions, while at the same time constituting an important part of the individual's public existence. Equally crucial for the soul's relation to God as for the individual's religio-social status in the community, prayer (or, to cast a wider net, acts of religious devotion, like taking communion, writing spiritual diaries, reading biblical or devotional texts, perhaps even acts of charity) defined human existence from the closet to the political arena. This all-encompassing relevance of the interior (mental and private) and exterior (social and public) religious life is demonstrated by the papers in this volume. Their protagonists range across a broad social spectrum, from a Russian empress via British merchants to captives in colonial America. The key question, how to reconcile the demands of office, profession, gender and spiritual community with the kind and the intensity of religious observance expected by the self and by society, emerges from all the texts considered in the collection. In the relations between different Christian denominations, prayer can highlight contested ground, despite the fact that translations of devotional manuals crossed this divide frequently. Catholic veneration of the Virgin Mary, for example, was anathema to Protestants, so this form of prayer, if not totally rejected, needed to be reinterpreted and adapted for their communities. The functions of prayer were as multifaceted as its forms of expression, its genres, and its modes of publication. The papers elucidate all of these aspects, while concentrating on unique situations embedded in specific geographical, political and cultural contexts.

Mary Rowlandson's famous autobiography of her Native American captivity and delivery represents a religious prose narrative that straddles the realms of the private and the public in ways that were potentially problematic for a woman writer. While her text may or may not have been designed for a wider audience, the paratext – possibly added by Increase Mather – insisted on her exclusively private and introspective motivation which did not include the wish to publish. This is what Kohn regards as the 'cover story', justifying the publicizing of a private devotional act. As Kohn demonstrates convincingly, Rowlandson's use of scriptural quotations (above all from the Old Testament) proved her to be a skilful author who not only adopted an authoritative voice, mastering the sermonizing rhetoric of devotional literature, but who also used her seventy references to and invocations of biblical situations and motivations in various ways to express her experience and its impact on her spiritual existence. Rowlandson succeeds thus in merging a private history with a meta-narrative and in encoding messages she would not have been able to spell out explicitly as a female Puritan writer.

Elena Marasinova shows the far-reaching political impact that a single private prayer can have. When the Empress Elisabeth Petrovna made a secret vow kneeling before an icon of the Saviour, in a potentially dangerous political situation that might have jeopardized her reign or even her life, she might not have been conscious of the problems this would create for her in the long run. The precise words of the prayer are not recorded, and even the existence of the whole action has been doubted. But it is a fact that on the strength of whatever happened in the Empress's mind when she bowed – before witnesses – to the icon, she commanded all death sentences in the realm to be suspended. Such was the power of the sovereign's word as anointed ruler, and such was her conviction of the obligation to God she had incurred, that she held fast to her resolution until her death. The author argues, persuasively, that the supposedly humane renunciation of the death penalty (and its near equivalent, so-called political death) cannot be accounted for on the grounds of enlightened philanthropic beliefs, but was only due to a sacred vow made in a prayer.

Following the Deerfield Massacre in Massachusetts, in which Stephen Williams, then aged ten, experienced horrific violence wrought on his family, the boy was forced to live with the Native American perpetrators of these acts (themselves, as allies of the French, caught up in the ramifications of the War of the Spanish Succession) for a period of fourteen months, before he was ransomed. Having embraced the profession of a minister, it seems that Stephen Williams spent the rest of his life coming to terms with his traumatic childhood experience with the help of a spiritual diary that recorded his daily prayers over a period of sixty-seven years. Linda Menditz analyses in detail the forms of these prayers and their functions. She identifies ejaculatory, intercessory, narrative and preparatory prayers, all geared towards negotiating his place and duties in the world in view of God's grace and providence. Besides elucidating the relation between Williams's literary abilities and the development of his spirituality, the paper also reveals the significance of this diary as a source for the study of early modern prayer.

While a minister like Stephen Williams would find that the demands made on his social and public existence tied in perfectly with what would have been expected of his private, spiritual life as a devout Christian, the profession of the merchant seemed to suggest a rift between their professional and their religious lives. Financial interests and monetary pursuits might well be at odds with devotion to God, both in relation to the daily schedule as well as to the general purpose in life. While funeral sermons were often preached for ministers, and even for ministers' wives, the frequency of such sermons in honour of merchants was much reduced. Penny Pritchard finds, however, that the spiritual lives of merchants, when they come under scrutiny, were depicted in ways strangely at odds with their notably active professional lives. In the examples which she analyses, the passive Christian virtues were foregrounded in the merchants' lives: humility, acceptance, patience, faithfulness to contracts, trustworthiness, sweetness of temper, even if they might have been praised for their philanthropic engagement, or their active service, for example as churchwardens.

The papers by Laura M. Stevens and Sabine Volk-Birke take up the issue of trans-denominational prayer, looking at the complementing issues of translation, adaptation and reinterpretation. Worship of the Virgin Mary and by the mother of Christ was a key theme in Catholic and Protestant concepts of prayer. While the Hail Mary (particularly in its use within the prayer cycle of the rosary), seen as adoration of Mary, was denounced as an idolatrous practice by many Protestant writers and preachers, her own prayer, authentically transmitted precisely through Scripture and generally known by its Latin beginning, the Magnificat, shared a prominent place, together with the Our Father, in Catholic and Protestant prayer practice. Laura M. Stevens shows how the Anglican Church took pains to emphasize Mary's role as a disciple to Christ, rather than the immaculate Virgin or the nurturing mother. Gender issues were closely bound up with the positive or negative perception of Mary in any spiritual community, denigrating or highlighting such features of femininity as were felt to be suitable to the required interpretation of her role.

The Protestant adaptations of the Catholic devotional manual *Introduction à la vie dévote* by the early seventeenth-century bishop François de Sales also took issue with the foregrounded position of the Virgin Mary, here even supplemented by numerous references to saints and angels. Sabine Volk-Birke shows how its Anglican editors fitted the work for their audience and context by deleting many offending passages. Another key issue of the adaptation, however, was the attitude the

French source text takes towards mental prayer in the tradition of Teresa of Avila: a silent, even wordless form of communication between the devotee and God, which might be open to the experience of a mystical union. Protestant editors responded to this controversial issue in different ways, one seemingly not fearing that anything like this might happen to his readers, the other denouncing it violently in the paratext. The attitudes towards mental prayer in the Protestant Churches reveal different anthropological and theological concepts of the relation between the human and the divine.

These articles contribute to the development of the study of prayer in early modern society. They also help to define and characterize prayer. In these essays, prayer emerges as a capacious form of devotion. Prayer spanned the chasm between political events and individual piety. It also reflected the economic, geographical, cultural and religious contexts in which the devout offered their thoughts to God. In this sense, these essays argue for the development of the study of prayer as a broad and extensive field rather than a narrow one. For scholars to confine their study of prayer to those circumscribed by individuals, liturgies or denominations would be to impoverish our understanding of the ways in which prayer reached beyond these forms. In laying down an agenda for future scholars, this collection of essays suggests that prayer was such a central element in the lives of men, women and children in the period between 1500 and 1800 that it deserves much greater attention by scholars of history, literature and theology. Implicit in this is, perhaps, that it is an example of a field in which interdisciplinary endeavours can enhance our understanding of the past.

Notes

1. C. Columbus, '"Letter to the King and Queen of Castile" (First Voyage), 1493', in Myra Jehlen and Michael Warner (eds), *The English Literature of America, 1500–1800* (New York, 1997), p. 13.
2. A. Vespucci, 'The Medici Letter: Letter on his Third Voyage from Amerigo Vespucci to Lorenzo, Pietro Francescodi Medici', in C. R. Markham (ed. and trans.), *The Letters of Amerigo Vespucci* (London, 1894).
3. Scholarship on the rites controversy is extensive. Some recent publications include N. Standaert, *Chinese Voices in the Rites Controversy, Travelling Books, Community Networks, Intercultural Arguments* (Rome, 2012); M. Hu, 'Impossible Choices', in *International Journal of Asian Studies*, 4:2 (2007), 259–73; A. Chan, 'A Question of Rites', in *Monumenta Serica: Journal of Oriental Studies*, 44 (1996), 427–38.

4. J. H. Elliott, *Empires of the Atlantic World: Britain and Spain in America, 1492–1830* (New Haven, CT, 2006), p. 4.
5. K. Bross, *Dry Bones and Indian Sermons: Praying Indians in Colonial America* (Ithaca, NY, 2004).
6. Stephanie Schmidt, 'God in Ilhuicac, Christ in Anahuac: Encountering the Christian Deity in a Nahuatl Song-Dance of the Sixteenth Century', in *The Latin Americanist*, 59:1 (March 2015), 94, 95.
7. P. M. Erben, *A Harmony of the Spirits: Translation and the Language of Community in Early Pennsylvania* (North Carolina, 2012), pp. 229–30.
8. J. Craig, 'Bodies at prayer in early modern England', in N. Mears and A. Ryrie (eds), *Worship and the Parish Church in Early Modern Britain* (Farnham, 2013); see also R. Targoff, 'The Performance of Prayer: Sincerity and Theatricality in Early Modern England', in *Representations*, 60 (Autumn, 1997).
9. T. L. Lyons, 'Prayer Books and Illicit Female Desires on the Early Modern English Stage', in Mara R. Wade (ed.), *Gender Matters: Discourses of Violence in Early Modern Literature and the Arts* (Amsterdam, 2014).
10. *The New Week's Preparation for a worthy recipient of the Lord's Supper . . .* (London, 1775).
11. The first volume of the three planned was published as N. Mears, A. Raffe, S. Taylor and P. Williamson (eds), *National Prayers. Special Worship since the Reformation. Volume I: Special Prayers, Fasts and Thanksgivings in the British Isles 1533–1688*, Church of England Record Society, vol. 20 (Woodbridge, 2013).
12. R. Ginn, *The Politics of Prayer in Early Modern Britain: Church and State in Seventeenth-century England* (London, 2007). A. Lacey, 'The Office for King Charles the Martyr in the Book of Common Prayer, 1662–1685', in *The Journal of Ecclesiastical History*, 53:3 (2002).
13. See for example Bishop Hume's prayers written for the use of the Duke of Newcastle in appendix B of N. Sykes, *Church and State in England in the Eighteenth Century* (Cambridge, 1934), pp. 437–8.
14. P. Rogers and P. Baines, '"A Miser's Prayer" and John Ward of Hackney', in *Notes and Queries* 61:4 (2014), 542–5.
15. J. Maltby, 'Extravagances and impertinencies: set forms, conceived and extempore prayer in revolutionary England', in Mears and Ryrie (eds), *Worship and the Parish Church in Early Modern Britain*. L. Branch, 'The Rejection of Liturgy, the Rise of Free Prayer, and Modern Religious Subjectivity', in *Restoration: Studies in English Literary Culture, 1660–1700*, 29:1 (2005).
16. W. M. Jacob, 'Common prayer in the eighteenth century', in S. Platten and C. Woods (eds), *Comfortable Words: Polity, Piety and the Book of Common Prayer* (London, 2012).
17. A. Braddock, *The Role of the Book of Common Prayer in the Formation of Modern Anglican Church Identity: A Study of English Parochial Worship, 1750–1850* (Lewiston, 2010).
18. C. Ellis, 'Written Prayers in an Oral Context: Transitions in British Baptist Worship', in B. Nichols (ed.), *The Collect in the Churches of the Reformation* (London, 2010).
19. C. Garrett, 'The Rhetorical of Supplication: Prayer Theory in Seventeenth Century England', in *Renaissance Quarterly*, 46:2 (1993).
20. C. E. Hambrick-Stowe, *The Practice of Piety: Puritan Devotional Disciplines in Seventeenth Century New England* (Chapel Hill, NC, 1992).
21. N. C. James, *In Your Mercy, Lord, You Called Me: A Sung Prayer of the Christian Tradition* (Lewiston, NY, 2010).
22. E. Kraft, 'Samuel Johnson at Prayer', in *Religion in the Age of the Enlightenment*, vol. 2 (NY, 2010).

23. M. Rotenburg-Schwartz, 'Holy Land travel and the representation of prayer in the Enlightenment', in *Religion in the Age of the Enlightenment*, vol. 2 (NY, 2010).
24. R. Targoff, *Common Prayer, The Language of Public Devotion in Early Modern England* (Chicago, 2001).
25. I. M. Green, 'New for Old? Clerical and Lay Attitudes to Domestic Prayer in Early Modern England', in *Reformation and Renaissance Review*, 10:2 (2008).
26. S. Arnoult, '"Some improvement to their spiritual and eternal state": women's prayers in the seventeenth-century Church of England', in J. D. Campbell and A. R. Larsen (eds), *Early Modern Women and Transnational Communities of Letters* (Farnham, 2009).
27. E. Rapley, *The Dévotes: Women and Church in Seventeenth Century France* (Montreal and Kingston, 1990).
28. K. Gillespie, *Domesticity and Dissent in the Seventeenth Century: English Women's Writing and the Public Sphere* (Cambridge, 2004).
29. P. Mack, *Visionary Women: Ecstatic Prophecy in Seventeenth Century England* (Los Angeles, 1992); L. Laborie, *Enlightening Enthusiasm, Prophecy and Religious Experience in Early Eighteenth Century England* (Manchester, 2015).

ROWLANDSON'S 'COVER STORY': THE REVISION OF PRIVATE DEVOTIONAL PRACTICE INTO PUBLIC NARRATIVE

Denise M. Kohn

'This Narrative was penned by the Gentlewoman her self, to be to her a memorandum of Gods dealing with her, that she may never forget', explains the preface to Mary Rowlandson's narrative, titillating readers with the novelty of the publication of a woman's account of her captivity and assuring them that Rowlandson was a respectable member of the upper class who wrote her narrative simply to remember it.[1] The frontispiece to Rowlandson's *Sovereignty and Goodness of God*, printed by Samuel Green in Cambridge in 1682, gives another reason for Rowlandson to write her autobiography: to tell the story of her captivity and restoration, 'Especially to her dear Children and Relations'.[2] The frontispiece asserts that Rowlandson did not intend her work to be published; instead, the narrative was 'Written by Her own Hand for Her private Use, and now made Public at the earnest Desire of some Friends, and for the benefit of the Afflicted'.[3] The carefully worded frontispiece along with the anonymous preface entice readers with the promise of an unconventional story by a colonial author – a woman. The title and preface also create the 'cover story' for Rowlandson's famous narrative: she wrote her story as an act of traditional Puritan devotional practice.

Writing could play an important role in the religious lives of colonial Puritans, both men and women transcribed sermons, kept journals, and wrote narratives for self-examination and the edification of family members. The practice of remembrance – personal reflection upon the self and God's providence – was integral to devotion. In this context, the 'cover story' of the title page and preface reassure Rowlandson's readers that her text was an act of private devotion, not a public account of her captivity in 1675 during Metacom's War. By the time her narrative was published in 1682, the story of Rowlandson's captivity and redemption was well known in New England. Her captivity had been mentioned in histories of the war published in Boston by the ministers William

Hubbard and Increase Mather, and in London by Nathaniel Saltonstall, and rumours had spread that she had been forced into marriage with a Native American.[4] The publication of Rowlandson's narrative meant that she was entering the literary marketplace to tell her own history. In addition, she was also making literary history. Ann Bradstreet's *Tenth Muse* had been published in London in 1650, though colonial printers did not publish her poetry until 1678, six years after her death. As a result, Rowlandson is the first living woman to be published in the American colonial press, and probably the first female American prose writer to be published in the colonies. As a writer of spiritual memoir, Rowlandson was entering the growing marketplace of devotional prose, a genre that was even less open to Puritan women than poetry. The anonymous preface-writer to Rowlandson's narrative, probably Increase Mather, explained to readers that Rowlandson wrote only for herself and that 'this Gentlewoman's modesty would not thrust it into the Press'.[5] Fearing that his testimonial to her modesty and piety would not be enough to quell readers' criticism, Mather begged readers to '[e]xcuse her then if she come thus into publick to pay those vows' to praise God for her safe return from captivity.[6] Mather, whose many publications are a testament to his knowledge of the literary marketplace, was concerned that readers would view Rowlandson's text as transgressive, so he carefully presented her publication as the fulfilment of her debt to God, an extension of her private devotion, not as a woman's voice entering public space.

Scholarship on this captivity narrative constitutes a crowded arena, and a good deal of this work has addressed the question of its authorship. Several scholars have emphasized the role that others, especially elite men of New England, played in the publication and even composition of this text. Teresa Toulouse has demonstrated the way that Mather and other ministers appropriated Rowlandson's narrative to assert their authority and express their anxiety amidst the generational and sociopolitical conflict in colonial America and between Old and New England in the period.[7] Lorrayne Carroll argues that Mather's preface for Rowlandson's text initiated a tradition in which he and others wrote narratives in which they impersonated the voice and position of female captives, constructing and controlling female identity for their own purposes.[8]

All of these are sound reasons that help to explain why Mather and others supported the printing of her narrative. I want to focus, however, on Rowlandson's own motives, and argue that she wanted to publish her own writing for her own reasons. This task is connected with my emphasis on the importance of understanding this captivity narrative also as a piece of devotional writing that would have been read by its immediate audience as participating in a rich tradition of writing for spiritual examination and improvement. It was, in essence, writing as prayer.

This essay examines the ways that Rowlandson employs forms of devotional practice to create her own narrative, but it looks beyond the 'cover story' created by the frontispiece and preface to consider her autobiographical and literary impulse. Twenty-first-century readers primarily think of Rowlandson's text as a 'captivity narrative', a generic categorization that tends to elide the context of seventeenth-century spiritual writing from which her narrative arises. This essay will look at the conventions of Bible reading and devotional writing, especially as prescribed in popular Puritan manuals, to situate Rowlandson's work within the larger framework of Puritan devotion. Secondly, it will examine the ways that Rowlandson revises the conventions of private devotion and creates a public, oratorical and self-defensive style, using biblical citations as coded speech to validate her actions and sanction her publication. Finally, I argue that Rowlandson's transformation of private devotional practice into public narrative suggests that ultimately she wrote for a public audience much larger than the small circle of her children and relations asserted by the 'cover story' of the frontispiece and preface. While we can never really know her intentions as a writer, the evidence that she was writing a private narrative is from the cover and preface. The fact that the frontispiece and preface validate her text via cultural norms of feminine privacy and reticence does not mean that readers should accept the belief that she sought privacy and reticence – especially when the evidence of her narrative suggests otherwise. The 'cover story' needed to proclaim her modesty to validate her text, especially within the context of rumours that Rowlandson, the wife of a Puritan minister, had 'married' a Native American. Indeed, while Rowlandson's reasons for writing would have been multifaceted, one of those reasons would have been to defend herself as a 'Gentlewoman'.

Rowlandson and the Culture of Puritan Devotional Practice

Scholars have suggested that Mather or Joseph Rowlandson inserted or at least guided Rowlandson's use of biblical verses and sermonizing rhetoric in her narrative.[9] However, it is just as likely, or more likely, that Rowlandson included the citations and created her distinctive meta-narrative and oratorical tone without editorial guidance from Mather or her husband. While Rowlandson lacked the formal Harvard education of Mather and her husband, she would not have lacked the biblical knowledge or the ability to create an exhortative, oratorical narrative voice. She was immersed in a culture that venerated the literary as part of daily devotional practice, and as the daughter of a wealthy landowner, she had an education commensurate with her status. In the preface to her narrative, Mather saw no need to explain how Rowlandson developed knowledge or skill as a religious writer; instead, he focused on allaying readers' fears that she had engaged in unfeminine behaviour by 'thrusting' her narrative into the press.

Rowlandson's narrative arose out of a complex context of Puritan devotional tradition in seventeenth-century New England. The common practice of sermon transcription meant that church attendance was associated with writing. Men and women took notes during sermons, later transcribing them to read for their own edification, and interpreted and discussed them with family and friends. Meredith Neuman describes the production of sermon literature in Puritan New England as a creative 'discursive process that involves the entire community in the twined endeavors of scriptural explication and the material dissemination of that exegesis'.[10] Bridget Hoar Usher, the widow of Harvard president Leonard Hoar and wife of Hezekiah Usher, Jr. of Boston, was revered in New England for her faith and character and was especially respected for her skill in sermon transcription, a practice typical of women of Usher and Rowlandson's generation.[11] Parishioners could take on roles akin to editors and agents in the growing colonial press, bringing transcriptions of favourite sermons to printers. James Allin, teacher of the First Church of Boston, remarked in the preface to a collection of his sermons published in 1679 that the sermons were 'written out by some pious Hearers from their own Notes and by their desire hastened to Press'.[12] Thomas Shepard's popular book *The Sincere Convert* was published from notes without his permission.[13] Lay men and women were not merely passive listeners or readers – they actively shaped sermon literature by creating their own textual versions and discussing their interpretations. Such a culture gave Rowlandson ample opportunity to develop the scriptural knowledge and sermonizing style we see in her narrative. As a result, it seems reasonable to assert that Rowlandson wove the biblical citations into the narrative herself and created her own biblical applications and rhetorical style.

Rowlandson's frequent use of biblical verses as references to comment upon her own experience illustrates not only her knowledge of the Bible, but also the degree of familiarity that she expected her readers to possess. Like much of the devotional writing of the period, Rowlandson cited brief biblical verses, inserting them into her narrative without explanation of their meanings or the biblical context. Rowlandson's lack of explication of quotations is not a sign that she lacked biblical knowledge; it is indicative of her assumption that readers would have sufficient scriptural familiarity. Reading the Bible every year was a common Puritan practice: Maria Mather, wife of Increase, read the Bible twice a year after her children were grown.[14] Lewis Bayly's seventeenth-century devotional manual, *The Practice of Piety*, included directions on how to read the Bible 'once every year over, with ease, profit, and reverence', as did Isaac Ambrose's manual, *Prima, Media, et Ultima*.[15] Bayly suggested reading the Bible in chronological order to understand both 'the history and scope of the Holy Scriptures', and explained that the Bible could be completed each year by reading three chapters or Psalms every day – one at morning, noon and night – with six chapters left to finish on the last day of the year.[16] Ambrose emphasized the importance of understanding the 'drift and scope' of the Bible, including an 'analytical table' or outline of the books of the Bible for readers to review before they began their annual reading course.[17] Ambrose, however, was less prescriptive in his reading sequence, offering several different schedules and noting that 'every private Christian with a little industry' may devise a reading plan.[18]

Ambrose's manual demonstrated the way in which writing and reading were tied together in religious practice. In addition to annual Bible reading, he encouraged Puritans to write a commonplace book of special verses and 'such places as stare him in the face, that are so evident, that the heart cannot look off them'. He even included directions for the commonplace book, explaining that 'every Christian' can 'make a little paper book of a sheet or two, and write on the top of every leaf' a title to categorize verses by subject.[19] And he provided several pages of examples from a commonplace book kept by 'a weak Christian, the unworthiest servant of Christ', who despite his personal shortcomings, carefully records biblical verses under fifteen different subject headings, which include titles such as 'Places containing sweet passages which melted his heart'.[20] Ambrose's subject headings about 'places' of 'comfort' and 'sweetness' were similar to many Puritans' descriptions of their spiritual experiences, including Rowlandson's. For example, when describing the death of her eldest sister during the attack on Lancaster, Rowlandson interrupted the dramatic account to note that her sister had found great personal significance in the verse, 'And he said unto me, my Grace is sufficient for thee'.[21] Rowlandson explains that her sister had always described the verse as a 'sweet and comfortable . . . place' because it had offered support during spiritual troubles in her youth.[22] Later in the Nineteenth Remove, Rowlandson wrote about a 'Praying Indian' who expounds upon 2 Kings 6:25 as a 'place' that validated eating horse during times of famine. Rowlandson refers to 'comfortable' Scriptures twice in both the Eighth and Thirteenth Removes; Jeremiah 31:16 is a 'sweet cordial' in the Fourth Remove.[23] Ambrose's case of the 'weak Christian' who nonetheless kept a commonplace book illustrated the way that Puritans like Rowlandson and her sister returned to significant passages as 'places' on the pages of their Bibles and metaphysical locations of spiritual solace.

Some Puritans also kept diaries of daily temptations and providences as an integral means to fulfil the imperative of remembrance.[24] In a sermon transcribed by his parishioners, the minister Allin told colonists to 'keep up a Remembrance' of providences and be so focused in contemplation of God's mercy that they 'never forget them'.[25] In his *Christian Directory; or a Body of Practical Divinity*, Richard Baxter noted that 'some think it best to keep a daily catalogue or diurnal of their sins and mercies'.[26] Ambrose noted that many 'ancients' kept 'diaries or day-books of their actions' as a means of preparation for death and to help one account for 'God's dealing towards him, and his dealings towards God in main things'.[27] Ambrose's emphasis on 'main things' echoed Baxter's warning 'to not waste too much time in the ordinary accounts of your life' but to instead focus on the 'extraordinary mercies and greater sins'.[28] As Charles Hambrick-Stowe notes, diaries were brief because the 'purpose was to record time, not to consume inordinate amounts of it'.[29] Baxter even warned readers that extraordinary events might be left unwritten: 'sins and mercies, which it is not fit that others be acquainted with, are more safely committed to memory than to writing'.[30] Puritans burned their diaries at the end of the year or instructed friends to destroy them at their deaths because private devotional practice was so intensely personal that it was meant to be used solely by the author. In the colonies, surviving diaries tend to have been written by prominent people, such as Cotton Mather, who wrote as much to instruct future Christians as he did to examine himself.[31]

Puritans usually wrote their diaries at night, Hambrick-Stowe writes, 'in conjunction with the reflective mood of nocturnal secret devotions'.[32] In Rowlandson's closing to her narrative, she wrote that she 'can remember' when she was able to sleep quietly throughout the night before her captivity.[33] Since her return, however, when 'all are fast [asleep] about me, and no eye open, but his who ever waketh ... my thoughts are upon things past, upon the awful dispensations of the Lord towards us'.[34] Rowlandson's self-portrayal shows her continued alienation from her Puritan community after her return, and it also illustrates the logic of devotional practice. Puritan manuals strongly emphasized the importance of evening prayers and devotion; Ambrose wrote that 'when you layest thee down on they bed, then bring forth thy book, and take account of thy sins'.[35] Private devotion was considered the most 'powerful channel' for grace, and since sleep was emblematic of death, evening devotion was a marker of the point when the believer was closest to God.[36] Rowlandson could have situated the closure of her narrative in a different setting or without any specific mention of setting. But she specifically situated herself at night in bed in private devotion. She wrote, 'I remember in the night season, how the other day I was in the midst of thousands of enemies, & nothing but death before me'.[37] She chose to dramatize herself 'as weeping' while others 'are sleeping'; like David, she says, at night she 'waters her couch with her tears'.[38] Rowlandson emphasized the paradigms of devotional structures, using the practice of regular, evening devotion as a closing frame for her narrative.

Rowlandson's emphasis on evening devotion linked her narrative to spiritual autobiography, which Puritans were most likely to write when they faced death. In *A Christian's Daily Walk*, Henry Scudder reminded readers that 'when you lie down, you may think of lying down in your winding-sheet, and in your grave'.[39] Most spiritual autobiographies were written as accounts to be shared with family and friends at the author's death. The best-known spiritual autobiographies by American Puritans are those of Anne Bradstreet, John Dane and Sarah Goodhue. Bradstreet related her personal 'experiences of God's gracious dealings' in her letter 'To My Dear Children', written around 1672 when she was ill and feared that she would be unable to share her memories on her deathbed.[40] Dane, a tailor, wrote his 'Declarations of the Remarkable Providences in the Course of My Life' for his family in 1682, when he was seventy, out of concern that he might soon die. Sarah Goodhue, who feared she would die in childbirth, exhorted her family and friends to be faithful in case 'God in his Providence' should 'begin by death to break you'.[41] These narratives are typical of the brief memoirs written during Rowlandson's period: personal accounts written for a private audience. The narratives of Bradstreet and Dane were also kept private by their family and friends; Dane's account was first printed in 1854 and Bradstreet's in 1867. Scholars are unsure whether Goodhue's account was first printed in 1681 by Samuel Green, who also published Rowlandson, but it seems more likely that it was first published a century later, in 1770.

The fact that for many years scholars believed that Rowlandson died soon after the publication of her narrative suggests the extent to which her story was read within the genre of the 'deathbed' spiritual memoir. While Rowlandson's narrative arises out of the spiritual imperative for remembrance, Rowlandson was motivated to write by her survival, not out of fear of impending death. Rowlandson's narrative is also different because she never addressed her family and friends directly or indirectly as her intended readers. The only evidence that she wanted her narrative to remain within an intimate circle of acquaintances is the declaration that she wrote for 'her dear Children and friends' and the preface's statement that 'this Gentlewoman's modesty would not thrust it into the Press', neither of which she wrote herself.[42] Rowlandson's narrative also differs from these other memoirs in its length: Bradstreet's narrative is about 2,000 words, Goodhue's about 3,000 and Dane's about 5,000, whereas Rowlandson wrote about 22,000 words. The length of Rowlandson's story illustrates that she created a narrative that falls outside the bounds of the standard monitory memoir. It could be argued that Rowlandson did not need to stipulate a private audience of family and friends; such an audience was assumed within her culture. On the other hand, the cover and preface are so adamant that she did not write for the public that they betray a concern that readers would assume that Rowlandson had written for a wide audience and would disapprove of a woman who dared to share her private story with the public.

In her narrative, Rowlandson writes a public narrative that employs the basic model of Puritan devotional writing – the private recording of personal events and biblical verses that could be re-read to fulfil the imperative for spiritual remembrance. Rowlandson's narrative is a case study of the ways that seventeenth-century spiritual autobiography arose out of the literary culture of devotional practice. Lynch states that scholars have not fully examined the ways in which the 'formulaic stories' of seventeenth-century spiritual experiences 'both instantiated a model for imitation while also presenting themselves as quintessentially interiorized . . . Their repetition made an intensely personal and individualised examination of experience the basis of collective identity.'[43] Lynch's commentary helps to underscore that Rowlandson employed well-known devotional structures to craft her individual experience, and wrote her experiences to reinscribe herself as a member of her Puritan community after living among Native Americans.

Rowlandson's Revision of Devotional Literature: Meta-narrative and Coded Meanings

While Rowlandson's narrative arose from a culture of devotional practice and spiritual memoir, her narrative is different from spiritual autobiographies in style and purpose. One of Rowlandson's achievements is the creation of a public, authoritative voice. Rowlandson carefully crafted a literary memoir of her experiences with about seventy biblical references. Bradstreet, Dane and Goodhue each cited about three biblical verses in their texts, whereas Rowlandson consistently calls attention to the ways in which her emotions and actions relate to Scripture. While Rowlandson's biblical citations might at first seem like a Puritan afterthought or reflex, for her audience, these biblical citations would have created an intense experience of allusions between Rowlandson's story and the stories of the biblical heroes. The complexity of Rowlandson's narrative voice and her shifts between overarching biblical oratory and personal storytelling have been the focus of much excellent criticism: Diebold notes the tension in Rowlandson as narrator and character in her different 'colloquial' and 'biblical' styles, Derounian-Stodola examines Rowlandson's 'empirical narration' as a participant and her 'rhetorical narration' as 'interpreter and commentator', Downing notes the split between the 'vigorous and homely style' of Rowlandson's personal accounts in contrast to the 'elevated style' of her biblical citations, while Burnham finds that Rowlandson's 'stylistic dichotomy' results from 'her altered cultural subjectivity' from living three months with Native Americans in captivity.[44] Henwood argues that Rowlandson's biblical quotations were 'meditational signposts, directing us to ponder their meaning in the larger Biblical passages to which they point'.[45] Henwood illustrates Rowlandson's use of Psalms to reflect her emotional range, arguing that the 'doubleness' in narrative voice results from the righteous 'anger inherent in the devotional voice' of Puritanism and the Psalms.[46] In this essay, I want to build on the work of these scholars, analysing Rowlandson's 'doubled' voice as the interplay between narrative and meta-narrative and exploring new ways in which Rowlandson used biblical stories as coded speech to express emotions and opinions that she could not state explicitly as a female Puritan.

Rowlandson's text moves out of the realm of private memoir and into that of public, literary narrative through her 'doubled' voice. Much of the aesthetic pleasure of any autobiography resides in the interplay between an authorial narrator who shapes and comments on events at the level of meta-narrative and the authorial self as character who performs the story's narrative plot. Rowlandson exploited this interplay between commentary and plot with a creative tension and rhetorical flourish absent from other colonists' writing. She used biblical references as a means of self-validation, creating a meta-narrative in which she adopted the status and speech of male heroes through use of quotations from the Bible. Rowlandson heightened her alignment with Old Testament heroic speech through repeated use of the signal phrases, 'I may say like' or 'I may say as', transforming her experiences into those of biblical figures. About ninety per cent of the sixty-eight citations are from the Old Testament; only seven are from the New Testament.[47] Rowlandson's predilection for the Old Testament allows her to focus on a powerful God who displays anger and love toward an individual man who, though imperfect, strives to worship and glorify God, and ultimately attains a heroic status that glorifies the man himself. Although Rowlandson's biblical citations were brief, they were woven into her text as she commented on her experiences. As a writer for a Puritan audience, Rowlandson only needed a brief quotation to elicit a biblical story and its meanings. While sermons were founded upon the exegesis of a specific biblical text, ministers used frequent biblical quotations throughout their sermons as the major form of evidence for their assertions. Rowlandson, like a minister, used her biblical quotations as evidence for the assertions she made about her experiences; as a female speaker she cloaked herself in the speech of heroic patriarchs, thereby asserting the significance of her captivity. Moreover, her citations displayed her biblical knowledge, thus granting her authority to interpret her experiences. By embedding her narrative within the framework of the Old Testament, Rowlandson validated her story of suffering and redemption as a typological narrative of providential history.

The Seventeenth Remove offers an example of Rowlandson's appropriation of heroic speech when she speaks 'with' David's friend, Jonathan. Rowlandson wrote, 'Now may I say with Jonathan, *See, I pray you, how mine eyes have been enlightened, because I tasted a little of this honey.* 1 Sam. 14.29.'[48] At this point, Rowlandson had entered the 'wigwam' of a male 'Indian' and received food.[49] However, she did not express any disgust or view the food as 'unEnglish', as she does in other instances. So Jonathan's words suggest that she is so hungry that the food restored her, and that it tastes good. Within a biblical context, however, the quotation takes on an aspect of self-defence. In the story from 1 Samuel, Jonathan, son of King Saul, has eaten honey, which restores his strength and sight after battles against the Philistines. Jonathan, however, does not know that his father has forbidden his people from eating this day, even though they are weary. Saul is depicted as foolish for his ban on food, and he is clearly wrong when he calls upon God to destroy Jonathan for breaking his decree. Ultimately, Jonathan is saved by the people's outcry against Saul. For Rowlandson, then, Jonathan's words shielded her from readers who might have thought she was adapting herself to Native American culture and food, which might have been seen as a betrayal of her English identity. Rowlandson's 'honey' gives her the strength to survive, and she would have been foolish not to eat it. Her phrase, 'Now I may say with Jonathan' suggests that readers should hear their voices in unison, speaking together as she joins his biblical and her personal histories. Rowlandson's request that readers 'see' that her 'eyes' have been 'enlightened' asks for compassion from her Puritan community to understand how her suffering had increased her spiritual awareness. The sensory details of the passage – her eyes as enlightened, the taste of the food, the sound of her voice speaking with Jonathan – accentuate the dual spectacle of Rowlandson as the vulnerable captive and the friend of David. Moreover, that Rowlandson casts herself as Jonathan at this moment, the moment in the narrative when she entered a male Native American's tent and received food, served to elide her female identity and any suggestion of impropriety.

Puritans venerated David not only as an Old Testament king, but also as an author. In the opening of his sermon *The Times of Men are in the Hands of God*, Mather described David as 'the Pen-Man' of the Psalms. Urian Oakes wrote in 1682 that 'David after his great Fall Penned his

Penitential Psalm'.⁵⁰ Oakes's pun on 'Penned' and 'Penitential'– and the printer's use of italics so readers will more readily see the pun – call attention to the importance of David's role as a writer and his story of sin and redemption. For Puritans, David's narrative was crucial because it illustrated God's chastisement and love of the sinning faithful. In the same sermon, Oakes used Puritan belief in David's authorship of the Psalms as evidence that Solomon, David's son, 'Penned this Book of Ecclesiastes' after he awakened out of 'his Sensuality, Security, and Idolatrous Courses'.⁵¹ Solomon, like David, attains authorship – and heroic status – only after he has experienced sin and repentance. In his 1676 election sermon, William Hubbard referred to the author of the biblical book of Chronicles, which tells the story of David's reign, as '*the Penman* of this sacred chronicle'.⁵² In all of these examples, the role of a 'Penman' was associated with heroic authorship and was tied to the story of David as the supreme Old Testament author.

So when Rowlandson, a 'Gentlewoman' who 'penned' her narrative 'her self', clothed herself as the narrator in the mantle of David and company, she assumed a masculine authority that gave her the right to publish her story. She spoke 'as' or 'with' David the most frequently, on five occasions.⁵³ The first time that Rowlandson appropriated David's speech was in the Third Remove, when she and her wounded daughter, who had gone without food for four days, arrived in the Nipmuc town of Wenimesset. Rowlandson wrote:

> When we were come, Oh the number of Pagans now merciless enemies that there came about me, that I may say as *David*, Psal. 27.13, *I had fainted, unless I had believed, &c.* The next day was the Sabbath; I then remembered how careless I had been of God's holy time; how many Sabbaths I had lost and misspent, and how evilly I had walked in God's sight.⁵⁴

Rowlandson's explanation that she violated Sabbath duties served as her rationale for God's righteous anger. At the same time, her confession of sin was intended to illustrate God's love in sustaining her. In this instance, as is typical throughout her narrative, Rowlandson used biblical references in an elliptical way, using what she has left unsaid to speak to her readers what she cannot say. The full verse of Psalm 27:13 is 'I had fainted, unless I had believed to see the goodness of the LORD in the land of the living.' This verse adds to the reflective commentary of the narrative; from her position as the author of her story, she looked upon the figure of herself as the suffering captive and asserted the constancy of her belief. The full verse also significantly alters her meaning. The partial quote, 'I had fainted, unless I had believed' stresses her faith; the full quote, 'I had fainted, unless I had believed to see the goodness of the LORD in the land of the living', emphasized her certainty that God will save her life and redeem her from captivity. For a Puritan woman to emphasize her belief would have been expected; however, to assert that she was certain God would save her from death even though her friends and family members had been murdered would have smacked dangerously of prophecy, and a belief in her own worth. By implying, rather than quoting, the full thirteenth verse, Rowlandson called attention to her special status as a survivor, as a chosen one, at the same time that she maintains an appropriate tone of humility. Even though Rowlandson repeatedly asserted that her experiences meant that David's words are her words, as a gentlewoman there were limits to the extent that she could ventriloquize an Old Testament figure.

Rowlandson's use of biblical verses as a means to comment upon her experience are too varied and complex for full analysis within the scope of an article, so two examples consider how Rowlandson used biblical citations to sanction her writing and publication. In the Thirteenth Remove, Rowlandson cited a verse from Job that allows her to validate the publication of her narrative. Before she cited Job, Rowlandson related how a Native American man said he enjoyed eating the roasted flesh of her son – a claim that she easily dismisses as untrue – and how she was temporarily blinded after a Native American woman threw ashes in her face. Rowlandson then stepped back from relating narrative events and provided the meta-commentary that 'Yet upon this, and the like occasions, I hope it is not too much to say with Job, *Have pitty upon me, have pitty upon me, O ye my friends, for the Hand of the Lord has touched me*' (Job 19:21).[55]

In this citation, Job entreats his friends and community, who have turned against him, to take pity on him for the afflictions sent from God. Rowlandson, too, asks for sympathy and pity from her community. She had been afflicted by the hand of God and this quotation was a reminder that Job's friends were unjust in criticism of him. In the next two verses of Job 19:22–3, Job's tone becomes more angry, as he exclaims, 'Why do ye persecute me as God, and are not satisfied with my flesh? Oh that my words were now written! oh that they were printed in a book!'

In alluding to these verses, Rowlandson condemned her community for judging her by suggesting her critics usurped God's power. More importantly, she justified her writing and the publication of her narrative through Job's desire to write his own story to explain his actions. While Rowlandson defended herself as an author, she also gestured to female humility with the statement, 'I hope it is not too much to say with Job'.[56] Her voice and Job's voice become one in this passage, allowing her to express her desire to see her own story printed 'as a book'.

For a final example, I return to Rowlandson's closing depiction of herself awake at night. In this passage at the close, Rowlandson employed David as her spokesperson. She reflected with anguish on her good fortune in safety and her previous danger in 'the midst of thousands of enemies'. She acknowledged that while others sleep, she is kept awake by thoughts of the 'awful dispensation of the Lord'.[57] Rowlandson wrote:

> The thoughts of these things in the particulars of them, and of the love and goodness of God towards us, make it true of me, what David said of himself, *Psal. 6.6., I watered my couch with tears*. Oh! The wonderful power of God that mine eyes have seen, affording matter enough for my thoughts to run in, that when others are sleeping mine are weeping.[58]

In this quotation from Psalms, Rowlandson slightly altered her phrasing of speaking 'with' or 'as', and yet the effect is similar in her claim to authority. She asserted that it is 'true' that experience made her 'thoughts of these things' the same as David's – her dialogue with David shifted from the oracular to one of interiority and shared subjectivity.

While the quotation from Psalms is important because it sanctioned her emotional and spiritual state, Rowlandson also quotes Psalm 6:6 to legitimize her authorship, as she had done earlier in her reference to Job. In Psalm 6, David negotiates with God, asking to be saved from death so he can continue to sing God's praises. In Psalm 6:4–5, he asks God to 'save me for thy mercies' sake / For in death there is no remembrance of thee: in the grave who shall give thee thanks?' In this larger context, when David says in Psalm 6:6 that 'I am weary with my groaning ... I water my couch with my tears', he cries, not from sorrow for his future death, but because in death he will lose the power to praise God. At the end of Psalm 6, David is comforted that God will save him, and he calls for vengeance against his enemies in Psalm 6:10, 'Let all my enemies be ashamed and sore vexed'. As Henwood explains, this passage follows Rowlandson's pattern of specifically quoting a verse of sorrow or humility that at the same time alludes to anger.[59] However, Rowlandson's use of this Psalm operated at a more complex level than an indirect call for vengeance. Rowlandson situated herself in a biblical context that sanctions her public narrative. David believed that God would save him so that he could praise God through the Psalms; Rowlandson suggested that she wept every night out of despondency that in death she would not be able to praise God through her writing. Since God had saved her, just as he saved David, so she must, like David, write her story as an act of remembrance and share it with others to praise God. Her salvation grants her the right to write and publish.

Rowlandson's Reputation: The Modest Gentlewoman and Rumours of Rape

Since Rowlandson was the first living woman to be published in America, her audience was not accustomed to narratives by Puritan women. Rowlandson's publication as a woman in a Puritan culture with a limited colonial press is as astounding as the narrative itself. That her narrative was published leads to the question, why? The answer was important to seventeenth-century readers: the title page and the preface answered the question. Scholars, however, need to think beyond the 'cover story' and develop our understanding of Rowlandson's autobiographical impulse to write. She had complex reasons for writing. Her writing arises from a rich culture of devotional practices and the imperative for remembrance. In addition, as Derounian-Stodola has shown, Rowlandson may have written her narrative to cope with the trauma of captivity.[60] It also seems likely, as Derounian-Stodola has shown, that Mather wrote the preface and helped in the publication of the narrative as part of his own interest in providential tales.[61]

I want to offer another possible motive: Rowlandson wanted to publish her story to defend herself against charges that she had married a Native American sachem while in captivity. There is enough information in the narrative and the historical context of its publication to make this explanation plausible. The suggestion that Rowlandson sought to defend her reputation against charges that she had consensual sex or was raped by a Native American and sought publication in transatlantic print culture do not contradict the other reasons to write and publish; indeed, I would argue that this explanation helps to bolster what we already know by providing a fuller, more complex version of Rowlandson.

Rowlandson was the most prominent political prisoner in Metacom's War, a time of great concern over backsliding among the faithful in the colonies. Her captivity was included in most contemporary accounts of Metacom's War published in New England and London even before her own narrative was printed; so whether or not she wanted public attention, she was already famous. By the time her narrative was printed, readers on both sides of the Atlantic knew she was a minister's wife who had been kidnapped, held captive, and redeemed. However, rumours had circulated that she had been forced to 'marry' Monoco, the Nipmuc sachem who led the attack on Lancaster. Nathaniel Saltonstall, who published three chronicles of Metacom's War in London from 1675–6, stated in his final account that

> There was a Report that they [Native Americans] had forced Mrs. Rowlinson to marry the one eyed Sachem, but it was soon contradicted; for being a very pious Woman and of great Faith, the Lord wonderfully supported her under this Affliction, so that she appeared and behaved her self amongst them with so much Courage and majestick Gravity, that none durst offer any Violence to her, but on the contrary (in their rude manner) seemed show her great Respect[.][62]

Although Saltonstall related the rumour to discredit it, he was, of course, spreading the sensational 'Report' across the Atlantic and importing it back to the colonies via the book trade. Although Saltonstall wrote that the report of forced marriage was 'soon contradicted', he did not declare the report to be malicious, slanderous or false. In addition, Saltonstall related the tale of Rowlandson's forced marriage immediately after describing the murder of her sister-in-law, contrasting the fates of the two women. Rowlandson received 'great Respect', which she had earned through God's help and her own behaviour; her sister-in-law did not share her good fortune. In harrowing and spurious detail, Saltonstall wrote that the Native Americans followed Rowlandson's pregnant sister-in-law into the woods and 'in a jeering Manner' offered to be her 'Midwives' as they 'barbarously ript up her Body, burnt the Child before her Face, and then in a merciful Cruelty, to put her out of pain, knockt her o'th Head'.[63] Saltonstall's account of the violent brutality of the Native Americans seemed to add weight to, rather than discredit, the possibility of a 'forced' marriage. Indeed, Saltonstall was eager to sensationalize the war, and spread false stories of Native Americans raping female colonists. In his first published account of Metacom's War, Saltonstall claimed that Native Americans 'defiled' a woman in Swansea before killing her in June 1675 and also that captured women were raped before they were killed.[64] Saltonstall asserted that the 'Heathen rarely giv[e] Quarter to those that they take, but if they were Women, they first forced them to satisifie their filthy Lusts and then murdered them'.[65]

Although records show that rape was part of English culture, it was not part of Native American culture, even in war.[66] Allegations of rape were racist propaganda intended to heighten colonial fear-mongering and counter support for Christian Native Americans during the war. Saltonstall's 'Report' and then rejection of Rowlandson's 'forced' marriage played into fears of social and sexual relationships between colonists and Native Americans as transgressions of cultural identity, especially in a time of war. Rowlandson's use of biblical citations to legitimize her consumption of non-English food spoke of the importance of retaining cultural identity even in the necessities of survival. In addition, allegations of sexual violence projected colonists' fears about their own moral declension on their enemies. The sermons of the period are a testament to the colonists' anxiety that they were losing the faith and morality of their fathers' generation; and a wartime climate of uncertainty may have prompted a renewed interest in prosecuting those who were seen as immoral. Court records in Middlesex County show a sharp rise in fornication cases during the war and also in the number of cases in which fathers prosecuted young men for having sex with their unmarried daughters.[67] Magistrates and ministers complained that military parades and musters promoted frivolity and drinking.[68]

Saltonstall's allegations of Rowlandson's forced marriage have long been part of our knowledge about Rowlandson's history; Diebold and Salisbury both discuss the allegations of rape, and Faery is exceptional in considering the allegations as a motive for Rowlandson's writing.[69] In general, though, scholarship has tended to overlook Saltonstall's account as crucial to Rowlandson's autobiographical impulse. Perhaps scholars have been dismissive of the allegations because it is known stories of Native Americans rape are false. However, even though the rumours were spurious, we should not dismiss the effect that false allegations and the ensuing innuendo had for Rowlandson. Saltonstall's statement that there 'was a Report that they had forced Mrs. Rowlinson to marry the one eyed Sachem' is more complex than his accounts that women had been 'defiled'. Being 'forced' to marry denotes rape – Saltonstall was probably using careful phrasing rather than the more explicit term 'defiled' out of respect for Rowlandson and her husband. Yet, Saltonstall's phrasing also allowed for ambiguity. Besides denoting rape, the phrase 'forced' to marry also suggested the possibility that Rowlandson had become one of Monoco's wives and an adopted member of the Native American community. In addition, the phrase that '*they* had forced Mrs. Rowlinson to marry the one eyed *Sachem*' (emphasis added) implied that the purported union was a community decision made for political reasons.

There is no evidence of English women forcibly or consensually becoming the wives of Native Americans and joining their tribes during Metacom's War. And, as Rowlandson's narrative makes clear, Monoco sold her and his right to ransom to the sachem Quinnapin, who was married to Metacom's sister and also to Weetamoo, the powerful female sachem.[70] My goal here, however, is to emphasize the degree to which Saltonstall's published account in 1676 spoke to the gossip that she faced in her community; and she lived with the knowledge that her experiences in captivity had become gossip in the transatlantic world. In the seventeenth century, rumours of rape, even though it was a crime, brought shame to a woman and her family. Furthermore, rumours that she had married a Native American or engaged in a consensual sexual relationship would have made her guilty of blasphemy, fornication, bigamy and adultery. Such rumours would make her husband, a Puritan divine, into a public cuckold.

Rowlandson addressed these rumours in a surprisingly frank manner, showing the need to deny the allegations. Though she repeatedly characterized Native Americans as barbarous, she asserted in the Twentieth Remove that

> I have been in the midst of those roaring lions, and savage bears, that feared neither God, nor man, nor the devil, by night and day, alone and in company, sleeping all sorts together, and yet not one of them ever offered me the least abuse of unchastity to me, in word or action.[71]

She also defended Native Americans against charges of drunkenness, which is incongruent with her need to portray them as uncivilized; but refuting charges of intoxication helped to defuse charges of sexual violence. Rowlandson told her readers that she only saw a Native American intoxicated when Quinnapin was drinking after a dinner during her ransom negotiations.[72] She wrote that Quinnapin 'drank to me' – a custom he would have adopted from the English practice of toasting – 'shewing me no incivility'.[73] Indeed, his toast would have been considered a sign of respect, and in effect, Rowlandson imbued Quinnapin with an 'Englishness' in this moment, as a 'civil' person, who although drunk, is not in actuality harmful. In defending Quinnapin – and the Native Americans she met against charges of drunkenness – she also defends her own reputation.

The preface to her narrative shows that by 1682, six years after Saltonstall published his account, rumours about Rowlandson were still circulating. In his preface, Mather wrote: 'To conclude, whatever any coy phantasies may deem, yet it highly concerns those that have so deeply tasted, how good the Lord is, to enquire with David, *What shall I render to the Lord for all his benefits to me.* Psal. 116.12.'[74] Mather's phrase 'coy phantasies' is a sexual allusion and suggests that colonists had enjoyed imaginative tales about Rowlandson's captivity. His syntax here, however, becomes uncharacteristically garbled, as if he cannot find the balance between acknowledging the rumour and maintaining decorum. In effect, Mather told readers that despite 'coy phantasies' about Rowlandson's captivity, 'those' readers who understood God's goodness would ignore gossip and focus on what they owed to God. In Mather's rhetorical sleight of hand, readers should dismiss the 'phantasies' to be considered faithful Christians.

In conclusion, Rowlandson made no apologies for herself as a writer in her own narrative, but in his preface Mather clearly acknowledged the problems of female authorship and belied his own anxieties about Rowlandson's reception. Apologia were conventional parts of prefaces, and even Mather, the most frequently published American writer in 1682, found it prudent to claim that he never considered printing his work except that God sometimes granted favours to 'those who are not men of skill'.[75] In another preface, Mather worried that readers would wonder about his prolific publishing, especially since he was 'the least amongst my Brethren'.[76] Mather's apologies seem formulaic rather than sincere – his professed humility is belied by his consistent belief in his own righteousness and authority. His apologies for Rowlandson, however, were profuse. He argued that Rowlandson would have sinned if she had not printed her story. In times of suffering people vowed to God that they would 'speak and publish his wonderfull works' if they survived, and Christians should fulfil their promises to God.[77] 'Excuse her then if she come thus into publick, to pay those vows', Mather pleaded, an admission that he realized a female writer needed a reason beyond remembrance and a public pardon for publication.[78] Although her name was on the title page, a sign that she had already gained fame as a captive and a writer of her narrative before her narrative was printed, Mather never referred to Rowlandson by name in the preface, identifying her only as the 'precious yokefellow' of Joseph Rowlandson.[79]

Since Joseph Rowlandson died in 1678 and Mary Rowlandson had married Samuel Talcott in 1679, the preface and title page hid her new identity as Mary Talcott. Her identity as a minister's widow added credibility to her words, but her husband's death meant that she was free of any concerns he might have had. The fact that her narrative was printed and bound with her husband's last sermon suggested that 'Mrs Mary Rowlandson' had died, too. Her new married name made it easier for her to publish her autobiographical narrative: Mary Rowlandson no longer existed. The obfuscation by the printer and preface about her name further attests to Mather's anxiety about her publication, and, probably, his efforts to shield her. Mather, however, also shielded himself, signing the preface anonymously as 'Ter Amicam'.[80] In anonymizing the preface, Mather exhibited an anxiety about endorsing Rowlandson as a writer. Anonymous prefaces were common, and writers often gave only their initials to the prefaces and dedications they wrote for sermons. Nevertheless, Mather signed his name to Thacher's sermon *A Fast of God's Chusing*, published posthumously in 1678; and the minister Benjamin Woodbridge signed his initials to his preface of Joseph Rowlandson's *The Possibility of God Forsaking A People*, published with his wife's narrative in 1682.[81] Mather, as a famous Puritan minister, in America must have known that his name at the end of the preface would have been the surest way to validate Rowlandson in the religious press. Instead, he chose to play it safe, adopting a Latin tag to show his learning and friendship while obscuring his identity.

Nevertheless, Mather's preface showed his regard for Rowlandson as a writer and the powerful effect she had on him as a reader. He invited readers to 'come and hear' her story, and repeatedly told readers that 'you may see' God's providences in her narrative,[82] underscoring Rowlandson's force as a writer of a text with oratorical resonance and visual imagery. As a reader, Mather supported her comparisons to Old Testament men, writing that her experiences 'bear some resemblance to those of Joseph, David, and Daniel; yea, and of the three Children, too'.[83] When Increase's son, Cotton Mather, wrote the captivity narrative of Hannah Dustan, he compared her to the heroines Hannah and Jael in the Old Testament, not to men. Cotton Mather's laudatory portrayal of Dustan and his references to Hannah and Jael can be considered celebrations of female agency that were made culturally possible to a great extent by the fame of Rowlandson's narrative. Dustan, however, would have been ineligible for comparison to David since she did not write her own narrative; in effect, Cotton Mather retained the role of heroic author for himself. The fact that Increase Mather did not appropriate Rowlandson's story as an author, subsuming it into his own prolific production of devotional and sermon literature, is perhaps one of the greatest signs of his respect for her as a writer. Moreover, Mather assured readers that they would find Rowlandson's narrative 'worth perusing again and again', thus figuring her public narrative as an appropriate text they could use for their own private devotional practice. In his critical estimation that the public would want to read and re-read Rowlandson, Mather also foretells literary history and the way that Rowlandson's narrative would eclipse his own devotional literature for generations of readers.[84]

Notes

[1] 'Preface to the Reader', in M. Rowlandson, *The Sovereignty and Goodness of God* (Cambridge, 1682), ed. N. Salisbury, Bedford Series in History and Culture (Boston, 1977), p. 65. Salisbury's text is based upon the edition published in Cambridge, MA, by Samuel Green in 1682, referred to on its title page as the 'second Addition'. Rowlandson's narrative was reprinted four times in 1682.

[2] Rowlandson, *Sovereignty and Goodness*, p. 62.

[3] Rowlandson, *Sovereignty and Goodness*, p. 63.

[4] See W. Hubbard, *The Present State of New England: A Narrative of the Troubles with the Indians in New-England* (Boston, 1677); I. Mather, *A Brief History of the Wars in New-England with the Indians* (Boston, 1676). N.S[altonstall]., *A New and Further Narrative of the State of New-England* (London, 1676), in C. Lincoln (ed.), *Narratives of the Indian Wars* (New York, 1913). Saltonstall reports the rumour that Rowlandson had been 'forced' to marry a Native American, *New and Further Narrative*, p. 83.

5. Rowlandson, *Sovereignty and Goodness*, 'Preface', p. 65. For the history of Rowlandson's publication and Mather's role, see K. Z. Derounian-Stodola, 'The Publication, Promotion, and Distribution of Mary Rowlandson's Indian Captivity Narrative in the Seventeenth Century', in *Early American Literature*, 23:3 (1988), 239–61.
6. Rowlandson, *Sovereignty and Goodness*, 'Preface', p. 67.
7. T. Toulouse, *The Captive's Position: Female Narrative, Male Identity, and Royal Authority in Colonial New England* (Philadelphia, 2007).
8. L. Carroll, *Rhetorical Drag: Gender Impersonation, Captivity, and the Writing of History* (Kent, OH, 2007).
9. See K. Z. Derounian-Stodola (ed.), *Women's Indian Captivity Narratives* (New York, 1998), p. 5.
10. M. Neuman, *Jeremiah's Scribes: Creating Sermon Literature in Puritan New England* (Philadelphia, 2013), p. x.
11. L. T. Ulrich, 'Vertuous Women Found: New England Ministerial Literature 1668–1735', in J. W. James (ed.), *Women in American Religion* (Philadelphia, 1980), p. 72.
12. J. Allin, *Serious advice to delivered ones from sickness, or any other dangers threatening death* (Boston, 1679), p. i.
13. C. Hambrick-Stowe, *The Practice of Piety: Puritan Devotional Disciplines in Seventeenth-Century New England* (Chapel Hill, 1982), p. 160.
14. Ulrich, 'Vertuous Women Found', p. 71.
15. L. Bayly, *The Practice of Piety* (London, 1719) p. 140. *Practice of Piety* was first published in 1611. See I. Ambrose, *Prima, Media, et Ultima* (Glasgow, 1757). *Prima, Media, et Ultima* was first published in 1650.
16. Bayly, *The Practice of Piety*, p. 140.
17. Ambrose, *Prima, Media, et Ultima*, p. 348.
18. Ambrose, *Prima, Media, et Ultima*, p. 350.
19. Ambrose, *Prima, Media, et Ultima*, p. 350.
20. Ambrose, *Prima, Media, et Ultima*, pp. 351–2.
21. Rowlandson, *Sovereignty and Goodness*, p. 70; King James Version, 2 Corinthians 12:9; all of Rowlandson's biblical citations are from the King James Version.
22. Rowlandson, *Sovereignty and Goodness*, p. 70.
23. Rowlandson, *Sovereignty and Goodness*, pp. 82, 90, 91, 78.
24. Hambrick-Stowe, *The Practice of Piety*, p. 187; K. Lynch, *Protestant Autobiography in the Seventeenth-Century Anglophone World* (Oxford, 2012), p. 10.
25. Allin, *Serious advice*, p. 7.
26. R. Baxter, *A Christian Directory; or a Body of Practical Divinity*, vol. 3, part 2 (London, 1825) p. 238.
27. Ambrose, *Prima, Media, et Ultima*, p. 139.
28. Baxter, *A Christian Directory*, p. 238.
29. Hambrick-Stowe, *The Practice of Piety*, p. 186.
30. Baxter, *A Christian Directory*, p. 238.
31. Hambrick-Stowe, *The Practice of Piety*, pp. 186–9.
32. Hambrick-Stowe, *The Practice of Piety*, p. 186.
33. Rowlandson, *Sovereignty and Goodness*, p. 111.
34. Rowlandson, *Sovereignty and Goodness*, p. 111.
35. Ambrose, *Prima, Media, et Ultima*, p. 139.
36. Hambrick-Stowe, *The Practice of Piety*, p. 156.
37. Rowlandson, *Sovereignty and Goodness*, p. 111.

38 Rowlandson, *Sovereignty and Goodness*.
39 H. Scudder, *A Christian's Daily Walk* (Glasgow, 1825), p. 139. *Daily Walk* was first published in London in 1627.
40 A. Bradstreet, 'To My Dear Children', in N. Baym (ed.), *Norton Anthology of American Literature*, vol. A (New York, 2007), p. 215.
41 S. Goodhue, *Copy of a Valedictory and Monitory Writing, Left by Sarah Goodhue*, in T. F. Waters (ed.), *Ipswich in Massachusetts Bay Colony* (Ipswich, MA, 1905), p. 520.
42 Rowlandson, 'Preface', p. 65.
43 Lynch, *Protestant Autobiography*, p. 123.
44 R. Diebold, *A Critical Edition of Mrs. Mary Rowlandson's Captivity Narrative* (Ann Arbor, 1972), p. cvi; K. Z. Derounian-Stodola, 'Puritan Orthodoxy and the "Survivor Syndrome" in Mary Rowlandson's Indian Captivity Narrative', in *Early American Literature*, 22:1 (1987), 82–93; D. Downing, '"Streams of Scripture Comfort": Mary Rowlandson's Typological Use of the Bible', in *Early American Literature*, 15:3 (1981), 252–9; M. Burnham, 'The Journey Between: Liminality and Dialogism in Mary White Rowlandson's Captivity Narrative', in *Early American Literature*, 28:1 (1993), 60–1.
45 D. Henwood, 'Mary Rowlandson and the Psalms: The Textuality of Survival', in *Early American Literature*, 32:2 (1997), 174.
46 Henwood, 'Mary Rowlandson and the Psalms', 183.
47 Downing counts 80 biblical references, p. 252; my lower count is for direct citations.
48 Rowlandson, *Sovereignty and Goodness*, p. 95.
49 Rowlandson, *Sovereignty and Goodness*, p. 95.
50 U. Oakes, *Efficacy of Divine Providence* (Boston, 1682), p. 1.
51 Oakes, *Efficacy of Divine Providence*.
52 W. Hubbard, *The Happiness of a People in the Wisdome of their Rulers* (Boston, 1676), p. 1.
53 Rowlandson, *Sovereignty and Goodness*, pp. 74, 90, 91, 95, 112.
54 Rowlandson, *Sovereignty and Goodness*, p. 74.
55 Rowlandson, *Sovereignty and Goodness*, p. 88.
56 Rowlandson, *Sovereignty and Goodness*, p. 88.
57 Rowlandson, *Sovereignty and Goodness*, p. 111.
58 Rowlandson, *Sovereignty and Goodness*, p. 111.
59 Henwood, 'Mary Rowlandson and the Psalms', 175.
60 See Derounian-Stodola, 'Puritan Orthodoxy'.
61 See Derounian-Stodola, 'Publication, Promotion, and Distribution'.
62 Saltonstall, *New and Further Narrative*, p. 83.
63 Saltonstall, *New and Further Narrative*, p. 83.
64 N. Saltonstall, *Present State of New-England With Respect to the Indian War* (London, 1675), in C. Lincoln (ed.), *Narratives of the Indian Wars* (New York, 1913), pp. 28, 30.
65 Saltonstall, *New and Further Narrative*, p. 9.
66 Diebold, *Critical Edition*, p. x; R. Thompson, *Sex in Middlesex: Popular Mores in a Massachusetts County 1649–1699* (Cambridge: University of Massachusetts Press, 1989), pp. 10–11.
67 Thompson, pp. 10–11, 36, 67.
68 Quoted in Thompson, p. 95.
69 R. Faery, *Cartographies of Desire: Captivity, Race, and Sex in the Shaping of an American Nation* (Norman, OK, 1999), p. 51. Faery also finds that Rowlandson's relationship with Quinnapin was 'erotically charged', suggesting that Rowlandson's tone was a factor of her own guilt for an illicit attraction. Salisbury also notes the Saltonstall reference and

considers that 'Rowlandson also wrote in order to clear her name with respect to a number of rumours and innuendos', p. 43. See Diebold, *Critical Edition*, p. x.
70 Rowlandson, *Sovereignty and Goodness*, p. 75.
71 Rowlandson, *Sovereignty and Goodness*, p. 107.
72 Rowlandson, *Sovereignty and Goodness*, p. 104.
73 Rowlandson, *Sovereignty and Goodness*.
74 Rowlandson, *Sovereignty and Goodness*, p. 66.
75 I. Mather, *The Wicked Man's Portion. Or A Sermon That Excess in Wickedness doth bring untimely Death* (Boston, 1675), p. A2.
76 I. Mather, *The Times of men are in the hand of God* (Boston, 1675), p. iii.
77 'Preface', Rowlandson, *Sovereignty and Goodness of God*, p. 67.
78 'Preface', Rowlandson, *Sovereignty and Goodness of God*, p. 67.
79 'Preface', Rowlandson, *Sovereignty and Goodness of God*, p. 64.
80 'Preface', Rowlandson, *Sovereignty and Goodness of God*, p. 68. Salisbury notes that the literal meaning of the phrase is 'thy three-fold friend', but in later editions it was printed as 'Per Amicum', meaning 'by a friend', p. 68.
81 Derounian-Stodola, 'Publication, Promotion, and Distribution', 242.
82 'Preface', Rowlandson, *Sovereignty and Goodness of God*, p. 67.
83 'Preface', Rowlandson, *Sovereignty and Goodness of God*, p. 65.
84 'Preface', Rowlandson, *Sovereignty and Goodness of God*, p. 67.

THE PRAYER OF AN EMPRESS AND THE DEATH PENALTY MORATORIUM IN EIGHTEENTH-CENTURY RUSSIA

Elena Marasinova

'Before the icon of the Saviour'

No execution took place during the reign of Empress Elizabeth Petrovna, from 1741 to 1761. The French diplomat Joseph de Maistre referred to this 'abolition' of the death penalty as 'false philanthropy and a sign of national inferiority'.[1] The Italian philosopher Cesare Beccaria, however, took inspiration from the 'renowned example of the Empress of Moscovia' and, three years after her death, published his work *On Crimes and Punishments*.[2] Catherine II also praised this act of 'our Auntie Elizabeth' as superior to 'the most glorious conquests',[3] and followed her example, making exceptions only for cases involving 'disturbances of the national peace', executing Lieutenant Mirovich and those who had taken part in the Plague Riot of 1771 and Pugachev's Rebellion of 1773–4.

This moratorium on the death penalty, unique in European history in the period, has remained without academic interpretation. Scholars have contented themselves with the account of Prince Mikhail Shcherbatov, who wrote of the palace coup of 1741:

> While making her move to take the throne of All the Russias, she vowed before an image of the Saviour Not-Wrought-By-Human-Hand that, should she gain the throne of her forefathers, none should receive the death penalty by her command for the entirety of her reign.[4]

This story, with some variations, is reproduced in all works devoted to Elizabeth's reign. Research into the circumstances of Elizabeth's suspension of the death penalty and of the ritual called 'political death' contains rich material for the study of prayer as well as the self-consciousness of the imperial person, for the channels of representation of power, mechanisms of social control, and the correlation between divine and state law in the minds of contemporaries. The subject is also a chance to understand the consequences of a prayer and the heightened religious feelings of an autocratic monarch.

Before the icon of the Saviour

Scholars have been sceptical about the authenticity of the scene portrayed by Prince Mikhail Shcherbatov. However, the French envoy at the Russian court, Marquis de la Chétardie, who had played a key role in the events of the coup of 5 December 1741, informed Paris of the circumstances of the transfer of power in Russia:

> On the 5th December, four thousand guardsmen received the sudden order to march out to Vyborg in twenty-four hours. [. . .] Elizabeth's party regarded [this] as intended to remove the guards from the scene, in view of their well-known devotion to for the princess. The [princess's] supporters persuaded her to decide upon carrying out their plan. On the same night of the 5th/6th, she first prayed to God, then sat in her sleigh and set off straight for the barracks.

Moreover, Chétardie names three witness of Elizabeth's prayer: chamber-junker M. I. Vorontsov, the surgeon Johann Lestocq and the musician Jacob Schwarz.[5]

The reliability of Chétardie's testimony is confirmed in the notes of Christoph Manstein, a Prussian major-general then in Russian service, as well as in the dispatch of the Dutch resident in Saint Petersburg, Marseillais de Schwart.[6] Moreover, the nineteenth-century historian and philologist P. P. Pekarskii managed to obtain an eighteenth-century manuscript, a poor translation of a foreign account, in which several facts were related. On 18 December 1741, on the birthday of the recently enthroned Empress Elizabeth Petrovna, the Russian resident at the English court had recounted the events. His account explained that Elizabeth's predecessor, Anna Leopoldovna, had decided to send the unreliable guards regiments out on campaign. On the evening of 5 December, a delegation of nine grenadiers had been sent to Grand Duchess Elizabeth Petrovna with the following plea: 'All-Merciful Sovereign! Deign to see the misfortune thou and all Russia now bear:

we are to be sent on campaign tomorrow morning, have mercy, do not leave us orphaned, but shield us with thy motherly vouchsafement from this plan!' According to the words of the resident, then the centre of attention at the English court, the future empress welled up with tears, asking everyone to leave the room, 'and herself, bowing her head to the ground before an image of the Saviour, pray[ed] in the secrecy of her own heart'. Elizabeth then appeared with a crucifix before her waiting faithful subjects and demanded their oath of loyalty.[7]

The Empress's prayer was no brief emotional impulse, though her promise, made before the icon of the Saviour, not to deprive a single one of her subjects of their life, contained no principle connected with the rational humanistic ideas of the Enlightenment. The impulsive actions of the Russian monarch before the coup were motivated, primarily, by deep religious sensibilities. Shcherbatov also noted that: 'Although it cannot be said that Elizabeth Petrovna was lacking a heart filled with philanthropy, the suspension of death sentences on her very accession to the throne were based not on any philanthropic system, but on religious devotion alone.'[8]

For the Empress, the image that had opened her way to power took on a sacred significance. In September 1742, J. S. Petzold, secretary to the Saxon embassy, informed King August III that:

> Last Thursday, there occurred for the first time, on the orders of Her Majesty the Empress, a nationwide church celebration in honour of the miracle-working icon that Emperor Peter I had had brought into his home during dangerous and important ventures, and which had been brought before the Empress on the night she led the troops of the guards out of their barracks and then took the throne.

Elizabeth created a cult of this icon of the Saviour, handing it for safekeeping to the Donskoi Monastery, regularly going with the court to pay reverence to the image and giving a diamond worth thirty thousand roubles for its casing.[9]

The anonymous author of the text entitled 'Anecdotes and collected customs and peculiarities concerning natural history pertaining to the various peoples of Russia, the writings of a traveller who had spent thirteen years living in this country' described also a formal promise made by the Empress:

Coming to the throne, she made a promise that, on the turn of each hour, day and night, she would pray to the image of the Saviour which was in her possession and hung at the head of her bed. There were certain old women whose duty it was to wake her on the ringing of each hour.[10]

If this account is reliable, it becomes clear why this icon found its way to the Donskoi Monastery.

'Sentences of execution and political death are not to be carried out'

The decree suspending the execution of convicts sentenced to death, political death or, in certain cases, even to eternal exile, was issued on 7 May 1744. The chanceries were thenceforth to send case descriptions to the Senate and await further instructions. This unprecedented decision was formulated without explanation and accompanied only by the remark: 'It is perceived that death sentences and political death not be carried out on either the guilty or the innocent'.[11]

Elizabeth was clearly displaying caution, which has led to multiple interpretations: on the one hand, it was ordered that 'executions not be carried out', while on the other, the numbers of death sentences issued were not restricted, and they continued to be pronounced as though nothing had changed. Even among the upper classes, few were told that the moratorium had been declared. The decree of 5 May 1744 was written in the Empress's own hand on the same sheets of paper as a resolution submitted to her by the Senate. This original was hidden, with a public copy that contained only the monarch's instructions that case notes for those sentenced to death be sent without delay. It was this copy, omitting mention of the secret decree, which was sent out to the collegia, chanceries, governorates and provincial administrations.

The preparation of extracts for imperial confirmation was entrusted to a specially created Senate group headed by the secretary Ivan Sudakov. Hearings of death sentences took place in secret: Senate minute-takers were not permitted to attend these sessions, and Sudakov's special group was given 'a chamber set apart from public affairs'.[12]

Observance of the moratorium required monitoring by the government and even the intervention of the Empress in some cases. The decision on the suspension of the death penalty was reiterated with regularity during Elizabeth's reign and gave rise to new renditions, clarifications and explanations. The repetition of the decree suggests the difficulties associated with its implementation, as well as occasional contravention, several instances of which reached Elizabeth and were reversed.

Thus, in 1749 the governor general of Kiev, M. I. Leontyev, informed the Senate that, despite the published decree, two Cossacks had been hanged in Zaporozhye for banditry and robbing the home of the Polish Jewish copyholder, Shmoll. The koshevoi ataman of the Zaporozhian host had referred in his report to the imperial ordinance, clearly known only to himself, to proceed with the executions, without which 'it would be impossible to eradicate thievery and other mischief'.[13] Not long before this, a similar paper had come from the chancellery of the Revel Governorate. The local Landraten and magistrate had asked the Senate not to abolish their 'ancient justice', urging that they be permitted to retain the privilege to sentence convicts to death without confirmation from the sovereign, justifying this by the increasing numbers of 'evildoers' on their hands and the difficulty task of feeding them.[14]

The position of Elizabeth on such attempts to change the decree remained firm: in all territories of the empire, without exception, 'those condemned to death and political execution are not to have these sentences carried out, case descriptions are to be sent to the Senate and a decree awaited'. No further instructions were forthcoming so the Senate was inundated with lists of convicts; prisons were full, and the death sentence existed only on paper. The Empress, however, was committed to the change. On the annexation of new territories, she immediately dispatched orders on the suspension of the death penalty.[15] The moratorium even extended to those convicted by the Secret Chancellery, and to military criminals. On 31 May 1744, the Senate issued the instruction to the agencies of political investigation and to the regimental leib-companies and leib-guards.[16]

As a result, in the ten years following the promulgation of the decree of 1744, 279 death sentences had accumulated in the Senate, and a further 3,579 cases concerning murder, theft and brigandage were pending, awaiting the confirmation of the Empress. 'The number of convicts grew by the hour' and jailers were unable to cope with their duties.[17] Catherine II recalled of the first few months of her reign that: 'The prisons were so full up of convicts that even though seventeen thousand had been granted amnesty by the Empress Elizabeth Petrovna on her death, at the time of my coronation on the 22nd September 1762 they still numbered up to eight thousand.'[18]

The problems which emerged from the implementation of the second part of the 1744 decree's statement 'on the non-execution of death sentences and political death sentences' were just as problematic. If the meaning 'natural death' was clear, the phrase 'political death' was not understood in Saint Petersburg or the provinces. Elizabeth demanded that the Senate should list the laws governing the ritual of 'political death' and indicate the crimes for which the punishment was incurred. Elizabeth received the answer: 'Concerning for which crimes political death is enacted, and on the particularities of this punishment – there are no precise decrees'.[19]

In an attempt to avoid Elizabeth's displeasure, the Senate mentioned several executions which could, as far as they were concerned, be understood as falling under the category of 'political death'. These had all taken place during the reign of Peter the Great. These executions had involved several common procedures: the 'utterance of death', 'lying on the block', and the merciful deliverance from natural death. However, the Senate's list was not comprehensive, lacking any analysis of case descriptions or sentences, and the examples were not termed 'political death'. The concept had appeared in Russian legal terminology, under European influence, in the notorious case of Peter I's interpreter, the diplomat and vice chancellor P. P. Shafirov.

The Shafirov Case

Shafirov was accused of 'contumacy against official decrees' in the Senate on 31 October 1722, and removed from his control of the post offices for twenty years. According to regulations, Shafirov had to leave the discussion, and was informed of the same by the ober-procurator Skorniakov-Pisarev. Shafirov, being a senator, refused to leave and called Skorniakov a 'thief'. Skorniakov-Pisarev opposed Shafirov, after which he left the gathering. Those remaining, Golitsyn, Dolgoruky and Matveev, were willing to continue the hearing, but Skorniakov-Pisarev insisted that the Senate session ended. Unfortunately, procurator-general Iaguzhinskii was absent, and Peter was away on a Persian expedition. Word reached the Emperor of the dispute in the Senate. Peter was incensed at the disregard for state decrees, the 'disagreement in the Senate', and the insulting of the 'honour of a place of justice with insolent bad language'.[20]

The sentence in a case involving such a prominent political figure called for an exemplary punishment. Shafirov was formally divested of his blue ribbon and sword, and condemned to death by beheading, having been reminded also of, among other things, his 'Jewish nature'. The execution was to take place on 15 February 1723 in the Kremlin, where a scaffold had been specially erected.[21] The Holstein nobleman Friedrich Wilhelm von Bergholz, then in Moscow, wrote:

> At around seven o'clock, I entered the Kremlin. Around the scaffold stood an innumerable throng. Once the condemned had been brought from the Preobrazhensky Prikaz on a humble sled, his sentence and crimes were read out to him. He was thereupon divested of his wig and old fur coat and taken up on to the elevated scaffold, where he knelt down and placed his head on the block; but the assistants of the executioner then pulled his legs in such a way that he was forced to lie down on his fat belly. The executioner then lifted a large axe into the air, but brought it down to the side, on to the block, and here it was that Makarov proclaimed in the name of the Emperor that the criminal, in honour of his services, had been granted his life.[22]

Shafirov had come very close to death. Stunned and tearful, he made his way down from the scaffold with difficulty, paying no heed to calls of congratulation. Such a balancing act between life and death by an important politician shook everyone, some sympath with Shafirov, as Bergholz sincerely remarked, a 'very honourable man'. Peter was very gloomy, receiving no one, remaining in one room and eating alone that day.[23]

Shafirov's case was the first instance in Russia of ritual 'political death'. From then, all such punishments, including those resulting from earlier judicial proceedings, were referred to using this specific term. Following the punishment of the cabinet minister A. I. Ostermann, who lay on the block and was subsequently pardoned in 1742, the term 'political death' became established in the law and was used in conjunction with the concept of the death penalty. In the situation of a moratorium on the death penalty, the significance of 'political death', as well as the detailed understanding of its procedures and ritual, would grow.

Natural death and its imitation

By the spring of 1743, the matter of the relationship between these two forms of sentence arose in a diplomatic context. The lengthy negotiations concluding the Russo–Swedish War were dragging on. Russia's international aims were no longer ambitious, and the position of Elizabeth, newly enthroned after the palace revolution, was not yet secure. Any political misstep might lead to an interruption of the signing of a ceasefire. Consequently Elizabeth was incensed when she was told of instances of marauding and even the murder of peaceful Swedish subjects by Russian troops. The situation was exacerbated by the fact that those suffering were Finns, to whom Elizabeth had promised support in their struggle for independence in return for their neutrality. The decision not to execute the marauders was problematic for the military commander, and also in diplomatic terms.

The solution was found in the concept of 'political death', which was used in communications to the Swedish chancellor. Elizabeth wrote to her Commander in Chief:

> Regarding the sentencing that all murderers and plunderers be broken on the wheel, and that the corporals and lance-corporals that permitted them to seek plunder be shot [. . .]; on this, our resolution is: that although they merit the most cruel death penalty for their evil-doing according to the laws of God and the ordinances of state, We, in Our mercy, do not wish to put them to death [. . .] and that you write to Count Schlenburg that We do not command these criminals to commit any delinquencies, and that We have not ordered them to be put to death, but declare that We have determined that all mortal crimes be punished not by natural, but by political death.[24]

Elizabeth tried to soften the offence of Swedish chancellor Gyllenborg, and of the local inhabitants, by ordering that offenders be punished 'there, where they committed their misdeeds, in the presence of Swedish deputies, to which, following inquiry, all booty is to be returned'. The sentence was made public and corresponded to the sentences prescribed by the General Regulations: 'Murderers proper are to have their right hand chopped off and, on having their nostrils slit, are to be exiled to Siberia, and those who have engaged in plundering, to be beaten with rods and exiled to three years' hard labour.'[25]

The decree of 2 August 1743 would have remained without consequences, had it not been for the 'terminological reverence' paid the Swedish chancellor. But the reference to 'political death', which sometimes included the lopping off of the right hand, as a substitute for the death penalty, gave rise to problems in criminal legislation in the eighteenth century; this led to erroneous conclusions in the historiography interpreting the moratorium on the death penalty during Elizabeth's reign.

The 1743 decree, composed for diplomatic ends and limited to marauding on alien territory in the midst of peace negotiations, contradicted the general moratorium on both political death and the death penalty. In addition, the form of public execution of insubordinate Russian troops that was presented in the decree as political death, but involving severing the right hand, did not correspond to the previously existing ritual of 'announcing the death and lying on the block'. The 1743 case would later find its way into a decree of 29 March 1753 and, ultimately, during the codification process that took place in the nineteenth century would determine the title of a decree of 30 September 1754.[26] Based upon this mistaken definition of the sense of the decree, some scholars have come to erroneous conclusions about the practice of replacing execution with political death.

In reality, execution and 'political death' were regarded as almost equivalent means of punishment, both of which were banned without imperial or Senate confirmation. Moreover, death and its public imitation in the form of 'political death' were so closely linked in the formula of sentences some confusion was inevitable. The problem of precise definition was difficult because both punishments remained only on paper. Consequently senators introduced distinctions between the two punishments.

In the spring 1746, a report was submitted to the Empress, in which it was recommended that:

> those sentenced to a natural death penalty, having been submitted to cruel chastisement with the knout and slitting of the nostrils, be branded on the forehead with the letter 'V', and on each cheek with 'O' and 'R' [*vor*, 'thief'], and those condemned to political death to be punished with the knout and slitting of the nostrils.

After this had been done, the branded convicts were to be sent away in chains 'to eternal heavy and constant labour'. The report also contains a description in general terms of the ritual of 'political death': 'if anyone is to be placed on the block or led to the gallows, and then to have declared to him the mercy of Her Imperial Majesty'.[27] On 9 June 1746, a decree was issued 'On the branding of thieves, bandits and other criminals with word *vor*, with 'VO' on the forehead, 'R' on the right cheek, and 'Ъ' [the Cyrillic 'hard sign'] on the left'.[28] Naturally, this was a form of indelible shame and the escape for those sentenced to the death penalty. The fate of those condemned to political death, just like the nature of the concept itself, still remained without imperial confirmation. The report was submitted to Elizabeth several more times, in 1746 and 1750, but imperial approval was only received in 1753.[29]

Scholars have suggested that Elizabeth kept silent for several years while patiently waiting for the senators to soften somewhat in their desire to 'compensate 'natural death' by an increase in physical tortures'.[30] However, the decision concerning the branding of 'VOR' was made without any delay. Senators urged that convicts should not be crippled but their labour used; this was not a matter of Christian mercy but of pragmatism and finance: 'the Senate makes so bold as to humbly state that those who have had their right hand cut off and nostrils slit and are sent to lifetime labour will not be suitable for any kind of work, but will only be a mouth to feed.'[31]

A detailed definition of 'political death' was only forthcoming in 1753:

> The Senate has determined that: political death is the term that should refer to such cases in which the convicted is laid upon the block or led up to the gallows, but who then is punished by means of the knout and the slitting of the nostrils or who, without corporal punishment, is condemned only to eternal exile.[32]

The apparent contradiction of this interpretation lay in the fact that some sentences of political death remained without being carried out, while the knout, mutilation of the nose and exile for 'theft and brigandage' were carried out routinely without report to the Senate, and were not regarded as 'political death'. Consequently, the Empress's ban fell not only upon the death penalty, but also upon 'political death', practically equated by the moratorium to a death sentence in its severity.

If the question of 'political death' was a problem of terminology and judicial theory, the actual suspension of the death penalty was a practical problem. There was the issue of what was to be done with the growing numbers of criminals who, while awaiting their fate, required guarding and feeding. The suspension of the death penalty had been signed, but all sentences remained, albeit without royal confirmation and without alternative punishment. In March 1746, the Senate reported that it had already received 110 accounts of murders, 169 case notes on thievery, banditry and other crimes, and 151 life sentences of hard labour. The senators suggested to the Empress 'that all of the above described be sent to labour at Rågervik'.[33]

The 'Rye Island' of Rågervik

'Rye Island' was the name given by the Swedes to a rarely frozen natural harbour fifty kilometres from Revel, which passed to Russia during the Northern War. The Emperor Peter visited Rågervik six times, personally conducting a survey of the depth of the harbour and taking the decision to construct a port and a stone embankment from the island to the mainland. In 1718, Peter attended in person the foundation-laying for the seawall and a fortress on the coast. In 1722–3 royal edicts were issued, 'on the exiling to Rågervik of those not willing to shave their beards and being unable to pay the fine' and 'on the exiling of schismatics to eternal labour at Rågervik instead of to Siberia'.[34] The number of convicts engaged in hacking away at the cliffs and breaking boulders would reach three thousand. Construction continued, but the plight of those driven to break stones for holding fast to the faith and traditions of their forefathers did not escape Peter. In his last decrees, on 26 and 27 January 1725, he commanded that all convicts be freed, except murderers and bandits, so that they might pray to God for the alleviation of His Majesty's sufferings.[35] On 28 January, Peter died. On 30 January, Empress Catherine Alexeevna, motivated by concerns for the soul of her husband, confirmed the amnesty to those convicted of less serious crimes.[36]

This imperial mercy and piety emptied Rågervik, and the port experienced labour shortages. By 1726, only 450 convicts remained at Rågervik, of which 150 would soon be transferred to the silver mines in Nerchinsk. By 1746, the Senate discovered that the island housed

> nobody, apart from ten artisans, and . . . the timbers having become unusable due to lying for so long in damp and poor weather

conditions, and the breakwater that had been built by the hard labour of the convicts, was now [almost half] submerged by water.³⁷

The senators recommended to Elizabeth that work be renewed on Rågervik harbour.

The Empress received the Senate's report in March 1746, and made a personal visit to Rågervik in July. Elizabeth was accompanied by the court, representatives of prominent noble families, the heir to the throne and his wife, Catherine. The young German princess hurt her feet on the island's rocky surface, and was, perhaps, the sole member of the party to notice the Rågervik convicts in her written account. 'The soil of this spot is stony covered in a thick layer of fine gravel. . . . The convicts working on the breakwater pier wore wooden clogs that didn't last any longer than eighteen days.'³⁸

Following Elizabeth's visit, the number of these 'convict labourers, working on the breakwater' increased markedly.³⁹ Convicts sentenced to death or political death were sent from all across Russia, with the exception of the governorates of Siberia, Astrakhan and Orenburg. Some Muslims, 'Trukhmentsy, Kalmyk and others', shackled hand and foot under the watch of 'the appropriate convoy', were driven to Rågervik from Astrakhan and Orenburg too. Women found guilty of serious crimes were regarded as unsuitable for stone breaking and so were sent to Siberia.⁴⁰

The harbour construction site had changed in comparison with Peter's day. The writer Andrei Bolotov, serving in the guard on Rågervik in 1755, described 'the honest or villainous throng' with whom he took daily roll call. They impressed him with their variety and confirmed the dictum that in Russia one can never 'rule out either the beggar's bowl or the gaol'. They were, Bolotov recalled, [people] 'of all types, callings and ranks: the well-born, there were nobles, merchants, artisans, clergymen and all manner of scum, . . . and apart from Russians there were people too of other nations, there were Frenchmen, Germans, Tatars, Cheremis and the like'.⁴¹

Having escaped execution and political death, the convicts nevertheless experienced severe suffering. Bolotov recorded that

> the convict labourers were led out to work surrounded on all sides by an unbroken line of soldiers with loaded weapons, they built their own quarters in a great fort, in the middle of which was a

47

huge chain, divided inside among the different barracks. These were packed completely full with miscreants, who numbered around a thousand in my time there . . . They were all clapped in irons that were never taken off, many of them with double or triple shackles.[42]

From 1753 to 1756, 13,242 inmates arrived on Rågervik, of whom 13,101 perished there.[43]

During the years of Elizabeth's reign, the Rågervik labour camp served an important function as a prison at a time when the Empress firmly upheld the suspension of execution. Although it seemed the practical aspect of things had been dealt with, an underlying conflict remained between the political elite and the sovereign on the matter of the death penalty.

'The Senate has great misgivings'

The Senate expressed its bewilderment in the autumn of 1743, immediately after the Empress had punished the troops who had violated the Finns. At Elizabeth's insistence, in May 1744 a royal decree written by her own hand on the suspension of execution of convicts was sent directly to the Senate, which further stoked passions.

The senators attempted to dissuade Elizabeth and put forward arguments against a moratorium on the death penalty. First, they stated that the numbers of criminals would grow. This army of villains would be very difficult to control, and prison escapes would doubtless ensue, disturbing her law-abiding subjects. Secondly, people, seeing the absence of punishment, would themselves become inclined to crime, and the army to insubordination. Finally, in the opinion of the senators, this dangerous form of mercy was counter to Russian legal tradition. They cited the firm governmental actions of the 'parent' of the ruling sovereign, 'the blessed and eternally worthy of memory Peter the Great', who had punished 'mortal guilt' ruthlessly. The Senate suggested that only death sentences be presented for the monarch's approval, and not those of political death. To all these suggestions, the Empress replied with the single instruction – 'that political death sentences not be carried out'.[44]

The opinion of the Senate was thus dismissed with ease in autocratic Russia, and the moratorium on capital punishment and on political death was rigorously enforced. However, the ideas behind the Senate's suggestions were revealed in the composition of the unfinished text of the new law code.

In August 1754, on the motion of the senator P. I. Shuvalov, a specially convened Senate commission sat for the 'composition of clear and understandable laws'. The commission's task was to propose a future law code, comprising four parts: 'on the courts', 'on the various conditions of subjects', 'on moveable and fixed property', and 'on executions, punishments and fines'.[45] The 'justice' and 'criminal' sections were completed in a year. But Elizabeth did not respond to them until 1759, after which she ordered the text to be revised and the two other parts completed. The commission was reinforced by the addition of the senators Roman Vorontsov and Mikhail Shakhovskii,[46] and in 1761 the Empress received the 'arguments previous to the commission' and matters as 'reasoned by the present commission'.

The revised articles, on the one hand, represented a continuity with the Code of Law of 1649, Military Articles of 1716, Naval Regulations of 1720 and General Regulations of 1720, and, on the other, ignored the decrees issued by the Empress concerning the death penalty and political death. After a decade of a moratorium on executions, death penalty was extended, and the process of execution made harsher. According to the commission, the death penalty should continue to apply to convicted bandits, murderers and forgers and would also include those who had stolen over forty roubles, thieves convicted for the third time, importers of coins, grave robbers and those damaging another's health, as well as governors or military commanders who failed to promulgate decrees intended for the public.[47] The death penalty was proposed as the sentence for a wide spectrum of crimes against religion, the Church, the state and public order, for murder, theft, banditry, smuggling, witchcraft, fornication, complicity and failure to report a crime.

Among the proposed methods of execution, a convict might be beheaded, quartered, hung by the rib, burnt, have molten lead poured down his throat, or even be torn apart by five horses, which was unknown in the Russian tradition.[48]

The proposed new law code therefore did not soften the criminal code. As for imperial confirmation of sentences, the Senate proposed a reduction in the level at which sentences were subject to approval. It was proposed that the fate of noble and mercantile criminals would be decided by the Senate, while that of 'base-born and common villains' would be determined by the governorate or the College of Justice.

Following confirmation, the commission proposed that 'without any delay', the condemned would have two weeks for repentance, take communion, and on a subsequent day be executed 'in an appropriate public place' not far away, with the crime of the convict and the fact of their execution being announced.[49] Clearly this approach was counter to the Empress's decree.

The preparation of the code was more remarkable since before work began on the project, cabinet minister Adam Olsufyev had reported that: 'Her Imperial Majesty commands that the death penalty not be inserted in this new code for those found guilty.'[50] It is clear that the Empress was unwilling to give way, and only her death ended this confrontation between the sovereign and the Senate on the matter of introducing humane punishments for serious crimes.

The 'renowned example of the Empress of Moscovia'

The moratorium on the death penalty was observed for over twenty years. The hypothesis, made by Shcherbatov, on the Empress's oath before the icon of the Saviour not to deprive a single subject of their life, has become the established interpretation. And yet the attitude of the monarch, the political elite and contemporaries towards the death penalty constituted an important element in the debate.

In Elizabeth's case, we are faced primarily with a crisis of conscience; Elizabeth turned to God for a miracle. A promise of piety was displayed by Elizabeth, who was 'undesirous of receiving interesting profits from the enemies of Christ'. Elizabeth appeared to take this upon herself as an obligation to God, in the event of Him granting success to her military insurrection. Since the revolt met with success, the debt had to be paid.

This religious sensibility could not be private because Elizabeth became the ruler of the Russian Empire. The coronation rite lent a special exaltation to the Christian faith of any Russian monarch, and the sacred will of the sovereign, of God's Anointed, was regarded as incontestable. The decision of the Empress to ban executions was based solely on her own relationship with God. Her subjects, including those whose fate depended directly on this decision, had no need to know of its existence. No decree on the moratorium, accompanied by explanations of the royal mercy, was issued. Only semi-secret instructions, not intended for 'proclamation to the universal acquaintance', were issued. The Empress did not concern herself with the fate of pardoned convicts, or of their salvation. They would die anyway, whether it was under the knout or the penal servitude in Rågervik.

Nevertheless, Elizabeth was uncompromising in her secret resolution. In line with her understanding of Christianity all were saved, not just the elect: nobody was to be put to death, regardless of the crime committed. The prohibition also applied to the ritual of 'political death'. The theatrical taking of life had also been part of the contract made with the Almighty.

Elizabeth Petrovna and Cesare Beccaria were separated by more than two decades, and Baccaria's enlightened ideals were not embodied in her moratorium. The decision was a combination of mediaeval religiosity and the belief that the law and the Empress's will were one and the same. The suspension of executions for serious crimes had no theoretical grounding, and was not connected in any way with the contemporary development of legal thought. The Empress did not aim to limit the public nature of executions to shift the emphasis from retribution to a triumph of justice in the courts,[51] or to move from punishment to prevention of crime, or other ideas from European philosophers and jurists.[52] It was the Christian commandment that led her to pose the question: 'who set me here as a judge over who should live and who should die?'[53] Having resolved that the best means of showing gratitude to God would be to refrain from employing the death penalty, Elizabeth forbade a single execution during her reign. A few months before her death, Elizabeth raised the question of a fundamental alteration of criminal law to bring it into line with the faith she professed.

Few attempts have been made to fathom the complexity of Elizabeth's motives. The twenty-year moratorium by supreme order became a reality, however, and prompted Beccaria to ask: 'whether the punishment of *death* be really just or useful in a well governed state?' In any case, it was precisely Beccaria who was the first to applaud the Empress

> who gave the fathers of their country an example more illustrious than many conquests bought with the blood of the sons of the fatherland . . . That some societies only, either few in number, or for a very short time, abstained from the punishment of death, is rather favourable to my argument, for such is the fate of great truths, that their duration is only as a flash of lightning in the long and dark night of error.[54]

Two generations of Russians never witnessed a death on the scaffold. The job of executioner gradually disappeared, as did the skills of erecting a gallows, and the ruling elites became accustomed to the death penalty existing only on paper, with the spectacle of public execution no longer constituting the main condition for upholding order in society.

A few decades previously, the bodies of criminals left out to hang as a deterrent to others, with tin plaques listing their offences, had been a familiar sight in the Russian landscape.[55] It was feared that uprisings and disorder might sweep the country if 'hereditary fear' was not sown in the minds of its subjects.[56] The first Russian procurator-general, Pavel Iaguzhinskii, proposed in a note to Empress Catherine I that one of the senators be sent to the provinces with the right 'to put [rebels] to death, and until this be carried out, there will be neither fear nor order'.[57]

The reign of Elizabeth primed the ruling and educated elite for a discussion on the utility of the death penalty, a shift that took place not due to any treatise by Beccaria, but as a result of the decision of Empress Elizabeth. The historian S. M. Solovyov wrote of this that:

> The people had to be weaned off the ghastly spectacle of the death penalty. The law abolishing it was not published: it is likely that Elizabeth feared an increase in the number of crimes committed once the fear of the ultimate punishment had been taken away; the courts sentenced people to death, but the sentences were not carried out, and so a great first step was taken on the road to popular enlightenment.[58]

Notes

[1] Zhosef de Mestr, *Peterburgskie pis'ma* (St Petersburg, 1995), pp. 85, 284–5.
[2] Cesare Beccaria, *An Essay on Crimes and Punishments* (Albany, 1872), pp. 97–108.
[3] *Nakaz imperatritsy Ekateriny II, dannyi Kommissii o sochinenii proekta novogo Ulozheniia*, ed. N. D. Chechulin (St Petersburg, 1907), p. 62.
[4] M. V. Nechkina and E. L. Rudnitskaia (eds), *'O povrezhdenii nravov v Rossii' kniazia M. Shcherbatova i 'Puteshestvie' A. Radishcheva* (Moscow, 1984), p. 55.
[5] P. P. Pekarskii, *Markiz de lia Shetardi v Rossii 1740–1742 godov* (St Petersburg, 1862), pp. 398–400.
[6] See K. G. Manshtein, *Zapiski o Rossii: 1727–1744* (St Petersburg, 1875), p. 250; Pekarskii, *Markiz de lia Shetardi v Rossii 1740–1742 godov*, pp. 425–6. In 1754, the French *Gazette d'Utrecht* confirmed the existence of the moratorium on the death penalty in Russia, which had been introduced solely as a result of a 'formal promise', made by the Russian Empress

on the night of the 'wondrous transition which raised her to the throne' (see *Arkhiv kniazia Vorontsova* (Moscow, 1871), bk 3, pp. 649–50).
7. Pekarskii, *Markiz de lia Shetardi v Rossii 1740–1742 godov*, pp. 431–3.
8. M. M. Shcherbatov, 'Razmyshleniia o smertnoi kazni', *Chteniia v Obshchestve istorii i drevnostei rossiiskikh* (hereafter Cht. OIDR) (1860), bk 1, p. 66.
9. *Sbornik Russkogo istoricheskogo obshchestva* (hereafter Sb. RIO) (1871), vol. VI, p. 442.
10. *Russkii arkhiv* (1871), bk III, p. 391.
11. *Polnoe sobranie zakonov Rossiiskoi imperii s 1649. Sobranie 1-oe* (St Petersburg, 1830) (hereafter PSZ), 12: 114, no. 8944, 7 May 1744.
12. *Rossiiskii gosudarstvennyi arkhiv drevnikh aktov* (hereafter RGADA), f. 248, op. 113, d. 919, ll. 99–100.
13. PSZ, 13: 25, no. 9586, 13 March 1749.
14. PSZ, 12: 583–4, no. 9312, 5 August 1746.
15. PSZ, 23: 576, no. 17264, 20 October 1794; 25: 622–3, no. 18943, 20 April 1799; 26: 786, no. 20007, 12 September, 1801; ff.
16. RGADA, f. 248, op. 113, d. 919, l. 18–18 (reverse).
17. PSZ, 13: 817–19, no. 10086, 29 March 1753. On this, see also Ye. V. Anisimov, *Russkaya pytka. Politicheskiy sysk v Rossii XVIII veka* (St Petersburg, 2004), p. 256.
18. 'Sobstvennaia zapiska Ekateriny II o pervykh godakh tsarstvovaniia', in M. N. Kovalenskii, *Khrestomatiia po russkoi istorii* (Moscow, 1917), vol. 3, pp. 200–1.
19. PSZ, 13: 819–20, no. 10087, 29 March 1753.
20. F.-V. Berkhgol'ts, *Dnevnik kamer-iiunkera Berkhgol'tsa, vedennyi im samim v tsarstvovanie Petra Velikogo, s 1721-go po 1725-y god* (Moscow: 1860), ch. 3, year 1723, p. 28.
21. RGADA, f. 248, d. 300, l. 271; cf. also ll. 263–6, 267–70 (reverse).
22. See Berkhgol'ts, *Dnevnik kamer-iiunkera Berkhgol'tsa*, ch. 3, year 1723, p. 28.
23. Berkhgol'ts, *Dnevnik kamer-iiunkera Berkhgol'tsa*, ch. 3, year 1723, pp. 28–9.
24. N. S. Tagantsev, *Russkoe ugolovnoe pravo: lektsii. Chast' obshchaia* (St Petersburg, 1902), vol. II, pp. 972–3; see also *Senatskii arkhiv* (St Petersburg, 1892), t. 5, p. 651.
25. Tagantsev, *Russkoe ugolovnoe pravo: lektsii*, vol. II, 972–3; see also on this RGADA, f. 248, op. 105, d. 8321, ll. 262–3 (reverse); f. 248, op. 113, d. 919, ll. 1–4.
26. See PSZ, 14: 235–6, no. 10306, 30 September 1754.
27. RGADA, f. 248, op. 113, d. 1023, ll. 11–16 (reverse).
28. PSZ, 12: 558, no. 9293, 9 June 1746.
29. RGADA, f. 248, op. 113, d. 1023, ll. 33–4.
30. See, for example, K. A. Pisarenko, 'Sekretnie protokoly Senata ob otmene smertnoi kazni, 1743–1744 gg.', *Rossiiskii arkhiv: istoriia otechestva v svidetel'stva i dokumentakh XVIII–XX vv. Tom XVIII* (Moscow, 1991), pp. 33–50.
31. RGADA, f. 248, op. 113, d. 1023, ll. 14–16 (reverse).
32. PSZ, 13: 819–820, no. 10087, 29 March 1753.
33. *Senatskii arkhiv* (St Petersburg, 1893), vol. 6, pp. 642–3.
34. PSZ, 6: 725, no. 4041, 28 June 1722; 6: 782, no. 4109, 15 October 1722; 7: 86–7, no. 4256, 28 June 1723.
35. See PSZ, 7: 408, no. 4638, 26 January 1725; 7: 409–10, no. 4642, 27 January 1725.
36. See PSZ, 7: 411–12, no. 4645, 30 January 1725.
37. *Senatskii arkhiv* (St Petersburg, 1893), vol. 6, pp. 639–42.
38. *Zapiski imperatritsy Ekateriny II* (London: 1859), p. 50. See, for example, other recollections of the court's 1746 visit to Rågervik island, F. Ch. Jetze, *Statistische Politische und galante Anekdoten von Schweden, Lief- und Rußland* (Liegnitz, 1788), pp. 92–7 ff.

[39] In 1751 alone, the number of 'those exiled convicts assigned to labour in Rågervik [was] around 2,000 persons' (PSZ, 13: 462-3, no. 9871, 31 July 1751; 13: 463-4, no. 9872, 31 July 1751).

[40] See, for example, PSZ, 13: 543-4, no. 9911, 28 November 1751; 13: 609, no. 9943, 23 February 1752; 14: 551-2, no. 10541, 12 April 1756.

[41] A. T. Bolotov, *Zapiski* (St Petersburg, 1870), *Russkaia starina*: appendix, vol. 1, pp. 341-2.

[42] Bolotov, *Zapiski*, vol. 1, pp. 341-2.

[43] On this see, for example, *Istoriia proletariata SSSR* (1933), nos. 13-16, 179.

[44] RGADA, f. 248, op. 113, d. 919, ll. 1-4, 5 (reverse), 10-10 (reverse); d. 1023. ll. 14-16 (reverse); *Senatskiy arkhiv* (St Petersburg, 1893), vol. 6, pp. 62, 642. On this, see also Pisarenko, 'Sekretnie protokoly Senata ob otmene smertnoi kazni, 1743-1744 gg.', pp. 33, 44-8.

[45] See, for example, PSZ, 14: 201-9, no. 10283, 24 August 1754. For details on the work of the Commission as a whole, see O. A. Omelchenko, *Zakonnaia monarkhiia Ekateriny Vtoroi: prosveshchennyi absolutizm v Rossii* (Moscow, 1993), pp. 39-53.

[46] PSZ, 15: 793, no. 11335, 29 September 1761.

[47] *Proekty ugolovnogo ulozheniia 1754-66 godov (novoulozhennoi knigi chast' vtoraia: o rozysknykh delakh i kakie za raznye zlodeistva prestupleniia kazni, nakazaniia i shtrafy polozheny)*, ed. A. A. Vostokov (St Petersburg, 1882), pp. 120-1, 143-4, 148, 171, ff.

[48] Breaking on the wheel was proposed, for example, as punishment for murder in the presence of the emperor, bandits were to be hung by the rib, counterfeiters to have molten lead poured down their throat, and arsonists and those failing to report them were to be burnt, and so on (*Proekty ugolovnogo ulozheniia 1754-1766*, pp. 68-9, 76, 92, 103-6, 111, 137-43, 143-4, ff.).

[49] *Proekty ugolovnogo ulozheniia 1754-1766*, pp. 54-7.

[50] RGADA, f. 342, op. 1, d. 41, ch. 6, l. 15. On this, see N. G. Sergeevskii, 'Predislovie', *Proekty ugolovnogo ulozheniia 1754-1766 godov*, p. xiv; O. A. Omelchenko, *Zakonnaia monarkhiia Ekateriny Vtoroi*, p. 42.

[51] The historiography is practically devoid of any comparative culturological analysis of the public spectacle aspect of the death penalty in Russia and the gradual decline of showy executions in Europe. It can only be stated that, in correspondence with the Code of Law of 169, the public aspect of executions, employed as a means of retribution and deterrence, was considered obligatory: 'Death sentences are to be carried out in those places where 'thieving people' have stolen or where they lived, and such thieves are not to be executed in deserted places' (PSZ, 1: 799, no. 431, 22 January 1669). In 1727, an attempt was made to regulate the ritual of executions to some extent. First of all, corpses and heads were removed from columns and spikes, and the remains of the criminals were buried. Secondly, it was forbidden to carry out executions in either capital, with punishment to be moved outside their boundaries to specially allotted sites (PSZ, 7: 824, no. 5118, 10 July 1727; 7: 859, no. 5155, 17 September 1727; *Opis' vysochaishim ukazam i poveleniiam, khraniashchimsia v sankt-peterburgskom senatskom arkhive za XVIII vek. T. II. 1725-1740* (St Petersburg, 1873), p. 101.

[52] On this, see, for example: M. Foucault, *Discipline and Punish: The Birth of the Prison* (NY, 1995), pp. 3-72; R. J. Evans, *Rituals of Retribution. Capital Punishment in Germany. 1600-1987* (Oxford, 1996), pp. 130-7, etc.; H.-J. Graff, 'Crime and Punishment in the Nineteenth Century: a New Look at the Criminal', *Journal of Interdisciplinary History*, 7:3 (Winter 1977), 477-91; J. Martschukat, *Inszeniertes Töten: Eine Geschichte der Todesstrafe vom 17. Bis zum 19. Jahrhundert* (Köln, 2000), pp. 12-53.

53 It is characteristic that the members of the Synod, even when in full agreement with the sentence, had no right to sign a death sentence, 'in so far as they belong essentially to a clerical rank' (see, for instance PSZ, 16: 906–7, no. 12241, 15 September 1764).

54 Cesare Beccaria, *An Essay on Crimes and Punishments*, pp. 98–107.

55 In the January of 1726, it was therefore ordered that the commissioners of the Obonezhskaia Piatina in the Province of Novgorod, Nikita Artsybashev, Grigory Baranov and subdeacon Iakov Volotskii, be 'hanged in the same Obonezhkaia Piatina, with their guilt written on placards nailed to the gallows, and that their bodies not be taken down from these gallows'. Their crime, carried out in this way in the sight of all the inhabitants, consisted of taking bribes and embezzling public funds, particularly in the purchase of loaves on means taken from the recruitment collections and making use of the proceeds without paying the requisite fees (PSZ, 7, no. 4826, 24 January 1726).

56 S. M. Solovyov, *Istoriia Rossii s drevneishikh vremen* (Moscow, 1964), bk X, vols 19–20, p. 608.

57 'Zapiski P. I. Iaguzhinskogo o sostoianii Rossii', Cht. OIDR (1860), bk 4, p. 271.

58 Solovyov, *Istoriia Rossii s drevneishikh vremen*, book XI, vols 21–2, p. 527.

THE CAPTIVE AT PRAYER: CROSS-CULTURAL TRAUMA AS REVEALED IN THE DIARY OF STEPHEN WILLIAMS

Linda Meditz

My story begins with a ten-year-old boy caught in the crossfire of European conflict played out on the New England frontier at the dawn of the eighteenth century. On 29 February 1704, Stephen Williams was asleep in his bed as French and Indian forces converged on the tiny English settlement of Deerfield, Massachusetts and attacked the village. The town had seen the face of war before: a previous settlement at this location called Pocumtuck was besieged during King Philip's War in 1675 and had taken a decade to rebuild. This time the impetus for attack did not stem from regional conflict, but from hostilities overseas between England and France exacerbated by the installation of a French king on the Spanish throne in 1700. The War of the Spanish Succession (also known as Queen Anne's War after 1702) went on for ten years and spilled into colonial settlements in North America. To the north in New France, the French had built alliances with local Indian tribes, including the Abenakis, Pennacooks, Hurons, Mohawks and Iroquois of the Mountain. As a function of these arrangements, the French came to accept their Indian allies' cultural practice of 'mourning war', in which captives – often children – were taken to replace lost family members. In the case of Deerfield, 50 were killed and 112 taken hostage, in an attack long known to the English survivors and their descendants as the 'Deerfield Massacre'. It was one of the most lethal incursions of its kind ever mounted on the New England frontier.[1]

At the home of Stephen Williams, the impact of the attack was swift and severe. A group of over twenty Abenakis, Kahnawake Mohawks and Pennacooks entered the Williams home, killing some, and taking others captive. John Williams attempted to fire on his attackers, but his pistol failed, most likely saving his life. He was taken captive, along with his wife, Eunice Mather Williams, who had given birth to a baby girl just six weeks earlier. A slave named Frank was also taken captive; his wife

Parthena was killed by the raiding party. Altogether five of the Williams children were seized and two killed. Among the captives were Samuel, aged fifteen, Esther, aged thirteen, ten-year-old Stephen, eight-year-old Eunice and four-year-old Warham. Six-year-old John and six-week-old Jerusha lost their lives. Once on the march to New France, the elder Eunice Williams became too weak to proceed, so she was dispatched with a hatchet blow to the head. It is not known if Stephen witnessed her death. Early in the march north, Stephen was separated from his father and siblings. He spent fourteen months navigating the demands of life as a captive of a small band of Pennacooks, enduring physical hardships, including hunger and the near-loss of a toe to frostbite, as well as the emotional duress of separation from his family, as he and his captors pressed north and hunted along the way. In the spring of 1705, a ransom was paid for Stephen's release and the following November he returned safely to New England.[2]

Stephen Williams had much to come to terms with as he adjusted to life after the Deerfield raid. One unsettling aspect of the tale was the manner of death of his two slain siblings, Jerusha and John. In all likelihood, their heads were smashed against the door stone of the Williams house, their abandoned bodies in the snow among the last sights glimpsed by their grieving parents and siblings as they were marched away from town. For John Williams and his son Stephen, the 'braining' of the helpless children – a horrific but not uncommon incident of the Indian wars as raiding parties moved swiftly and eliminated those not likely to survive the trek north – was an affliction so grim as to remain unspoken. Writing about the attack in their narratives of captivity composed after the raid, neither the senior Williams nor his son Stephen acknowledged how Jerusha and John died. John Williams wrote sparingly that the Indians did 'carry [them] to the door', in order to kill them. Stephen merely said they were 'barbarously murdered'. Father and son alike struggled to see the hand of God in these brutal deaths. So close in age to John, and yet spared his brother's untimely demise, Stephen was at a loss to comprehend the ways of Providence. He was learning in the most graphic of ways that affliction – and the mercy that spared him – were bound together inextricably in the divine scheme for human affairs.[3]

In addition to the loss of the children, John Williams and his son Stephen faced the loss of wife and mother, Eunice Williams. Interestingly, both husband and son were more forthcoming in describing the end of her life. Heartbreaking though it was, her death was an event they could more readily comprehend. Stephen set the scene: 'we traveled about 2 or 3 miles [and] then they murdered my ever-honored mother who having gone over a small river [in] which water running very swift flung her down. She being wet was not able to travel any further.' John Williams wrote an even more explicit account: 'the cruel and bloodthirsty savage who took her slew her with his hatchet at one stroke, the tidings of which were very awful.' (It appears she was killed out of view of her husband.) Despite the violence, the bereaved minister found a measure of spiritual consolation. Just before she was put to death, John Williams was allowed by his captors to pray with his wife. Later, he portrayed her death in a spiritually edifying manner. Resigned to her fate, she searched the Scriptures for encouragement, modelling exemplary piety under the most dire of conditions. Unlike the deaths of the children, which were passed over quickly, the loss of Eunice could serve a greater religious purpose. Her piety and courage could be a model for others.[4]

With the long march to Canada under way, Stephen trudged along under the watchful eye of his captors and focused on his own survival. Yet he did not forget the trials of his siblings. Six months later, having safely arrived in Chambly (the gathering place in Canada from which the Deerfield raid was launched), Stephen's first concern was for his four-year-old brother, Warham. In his account of his captivity, Stephen described his relief upon hearing of Warham's survival: 'The French were kind to me ... They told me my father and brothers and sisters were got to Canada, which I was glad to hear of for I was afraid my youngest brother was killed.'[5]

The trauma of the Deerfield raid and his subsequent captivity laid the spiritual foundation for the rest of Stephen Williams's life. It was out of this crucible of cross-cultural confrontation that Williams drew the inspiration for his lifelong practice of prayer. While thankful for having been 'remarkably preserved' by God, Williams did not feel worthy of this distinction. He developed several modes of prayer in which he expressed this inner conflict – and through which he came to terms with other trying aspects of his early experiences. His rich library of prayers, penned in a sprawling spiritual diary of several volumes, constitutes one of the most detailed accounts of written prayer that survives from eighteenth-century New England and offers an uncommon opportunity to trace the spiritual impact of childhood trauma across adulthood and into old age.

In 1714, at the age of twenty-one, Stephen Williams was called to serve as a pastoral apprentice at the newly formed church at Longmeadow, Massachusetts. He was ordained in 1716 and ministered to the parish until his death in 1782. From the early years of his ministry, Williams kept two kinds of diaries. In one set, as was a common practice among learned men in New England, he wrote a line a day in an interleaved almanac about the weather, his travels and the affairs of his parish. The other diary launched by Williams was a spiritual one in which he made a daily entry for the rest of his life. Allowing for scattered gaps in the record, the nearly complete, ten-volume, 4,000-page diary Williams kept from 1715 until the last weeks of his life in 1782 has survived. Day by day, by framing each diary entry with various forms of prayer, Williams fashioned a remarkably disciplined and detailed account of his devotion to this means of his pursuit of piety.[6]

A survey of Williams's diary-keeping practice reveals the extent to which he used prayer to manage his spiritual anxiety and to make peace with his childhood trauma. Across the long decades of his life, Williams employed several modes of prayer to remember, reflect upon and cope with the painful events of his youth. In the first mode of supplication, known as 'ejaculatory' prayer, Williams dashed off a line or two in which he confessed his shortcomings and asked for God's help. The most striking aspect of this element of his practice is that he wrote these prayers down at all. Historian Charles Hambrick-Stowe explains that although such momentary supplications were often on the lips of pious New Englanders, they were conceived of with such a degree of privacy that their contents remain 'finally impossible to determine'. Williams's practice of committing these prayers to writing helps us recover the themes and language of this particular strand of eighteenth-century pious expression.[7]

In each case, these concise prayers represented Williams's complete diary entry for a given day. These supplications had a timeless quality – they did not begin, as many of Williams's entries did, with the phrase, 'This day', nor were they directly tied to any particular person or event. Thematically, his ejaculatory prayers often evoked the sense of inadequacy that dogged him from the earliest days of his ministry and that reflected a lingering sense of unworthiness reaching back to his childhood. Ejaculatory prayers from the first decade of Williams's ministry proved an exercise in confession built around the themes of pardon and forgiveness. For example, his entry for a fall day in 1717 reads: 'Oh Lord pardon my Sins – humble me for my amazing dullness – & unfitness for thy Service.'[8] A year later, he confessed untoward absorption in things temporal: 'Oh the cares of [the] world – again are upon me – Lord forgive me & convince me that these things are vanity.' Williams's brief petition on a June day in 1719 rehearsed the familiar lament of spiritual dullness and repeated the plea for 'pardon': 'This day has been a dull day with me. Oh – Lord – pardon the sins of it & make me serviceable to promote thine interest & Kingdom.'[9]

Over the next several decades of his ministry, Williams continued to craft ejaculatory prayers asking God to 'quicken' his 'Dead Soul' and to make him 'very carefull not to indulge Sloth – & idleness'. He also confessed to his ongoing preoccupation with worldly business: 'Be pleased oh Lord – graciously to provide me the things that are convenient – prevent my being overly concerned – about worldly matters.' The 1730s opened with Williams admitting he was torn between things spiritual and temporal: 'Oh Lord – give me to mind the main business – of life.' Three years later, the problem was getting worse: 'Worldly cares & business increase. The Lord grant I may not set my heart upon [the] world. Give me oh Lord – to refer all my concerns – to thee.' By 1737, his tone hinted at desperation: 'A world full of care & turmoil this is – the Lord be pleased – to wean my affections from the Enjoyments – thereof – & grant – I may mind – the one thing need-full.'[10]

Williams fashioned these brief supplications well into his old age. In 1756, having reached the age of sixty-three, he found himself feeling thankful: 'I am Surrounded – with mercies – oh what Shall I render to the Lord.' Several years later in 1762, the theme of his ejaculatory prayer hinged on his calling to the ministry: 'The Lord – help me to consider [that] his vows – are upon me – & the Lord be pleased – to help me to fulfill my vows.' When he reached the age of seventy-one in 1764, Williams evinced awareness of the process of ageing: 'I plainly perceive weaknesses & infirmities of age – the Lord be pleased – to help me number my days as to apply my heart to wisdom.' By 1778, having reached the age of eighty-five, Williams spoke openly of his approaching earthly demise: 'I am old – & infirm – oh that I might remember & realize it that my change is near – oh that I might give Diligence that I may be found ready for it.' In an overall sense, Williams's written ejaculatory prayers served as a brief touchstone with the divine across his long life – he embraced them as a form of prayer that allowed a child captive turned ancient pastor to offer an accounting for his many earthly days.[11]

Williams's ejaculatory prayers were embedded in his diary alongside a second mode of prayer: intercessory prayer on behalf of others. There were many people for whom Williams interceded: his immediate family and household, his extended family, his friends and peers in the ministry, and members of his flock at Longmeadow. Intercessory prayer also served to tie the pastor to his childhood trauma at Deerfield. Across his long life, Stephen's thoughts often turned to Eunice, his 'sister at Canada', who was eight years old at the time of the Deerfield raid and never returned from captivity. Instead, she remained in Canada, marrying a Mohawk man and converting to Roman Catholicism. She and her brother retained an affectionate bond through the years despite all that separated them. In the case of Eunice, prayer for her return to New England was the one avenue of agency open to Williams as the years passed and the likelihood of that scenario grew ever more remote. The language of Stephen's intercessions displays his ongoing concern for Eunice's return to the faith and family of her birth. Such prayers surrounded the return of Eunice and her family to Longmeadow in the summer of 1741. This was the second visit in two years; the summer before, Eunice had appeared among them for the first time in thirty-six years. On 26 July 1741, Williams received word that his sister Eunice and her family had arrived from Canada in the neighbouring town of Westfield. This news led him to offer the prayer: 'Oh that God would bring them to us – & reveal him Self in his Son in a Saveing manner to them.' The visitors arrived in Longmeadow the next day: '[I] found my Sister – & her Husband – & two children here – I am Glad to See them'. Williams then repeated the prayer he had written the day before that God would 'bless them and reveal him Self in his Son in a Saveing manner to them.' Williams still bore a sense of spiritual responsibility for his sister, whose life was spared, but whose soul, in his estimation, remained in captivity. When Eunice departed several days later, he turned to his diary again, writing: 'The Lord be pleased to bless my poor sister Eunice and graciously bring her and hers home to thyself and cause that she may long to return to us again.'[12]

When Eunice visited again in 1761, by which time they were both well over sixty, Williams was faced with the hard truth that she and her family had no intention of permanently returning to New England. Williams depicted this visit and its unwelcome news with a series of heartfelt prayers. He began his sequence of supplications somewhat optimistically, writing on 30 June that Eunice, her husband and daughter

Katherine had arrived, and asking that 'the Lord – Grant that it may be in mercy to her, that she makes this visit'. He next admitted to some frustration with certain aspects of the visit: 'we have no interpreter – & So can't Say what her intentions and profersions [sic] are'. Williams sent to Deerfield for an interpreter, seeking God's help in the matter: 'the Lord be pleased to direct me, and bless me – Grant I may take prudent measures'. As he waited for the interpreter, he also fretted about the untoward attention his sister and her family were receiving from local townspeople, writing on 2 July: 'People came in great numbers – to See my Sister – I am fearfull that it may not be agreeable to be Gazed upon.' The arrival of the interpreter only served to cement Williams's worst fears. He explained the matter in his diary on 7 July: 'I had a Sad discourse with my Sister – Husband & find they are not at all Disposed, to come & Settle in the Country. I am at a great loss to know what course to take, what measures to go into.' Again he expressed his worries in prayer: 'I do pray to God to direct me, & Show me my Duty.' What was his duty, Williams wondered, as the older brother to a grown woman who had forged her own path in life – one that precluded her return to the family of her birth?[13]

The answer is revealed in Williams's prayerful account of his conversation with Eunice a few days later. It appears Stephen was direct with his sister in trying to convince her to stay: 'I think I have used – the best arguments – I could – to persuade her to tarry or to come & Dwell with us – but at present they have been ineffectuall.' His efforts may not have produced the desired results, but Eunice was moved by them nonetheless: 'when I took my leave of my Sister and Daughter in the parlour – they both Shed tears and seemed affected'. Faced with resounding disappointment, Williams again phrased his desires for his sister and her family in prayer: 'Oh that God would touch their hearts, & Encline them to turn to their Friends – & to embrace the religion of Jesus Christ.' Having placed his sister in God's hands, and with a heavy heart, Stephen watched Eunice leave for Canada. He would never see her again.

In the twenty years after their sorrowful parting in 1761, Williams heard various reports about his sister's welfare. When word reached him that Eunice's husband had died in 1765, his first inclination was to remember her to God for her loss: 'the Lord mercifully regard my Sister in her widowed Estate'. He then quickly turned to his abiding worry over her eternal state: 'Oh that God would have mercy upon her soul – & Lead her into a saveing Acquaintance with thySelf . . . be pleased to

Encline her to return to her native land.' He was gratified to hear two years later that Eunice was 'alive [at] the beginning of January & She & her two daughters were well'. In 1773, word reached Williams that Eunice and her family were contemplating another visit to Longmeadow, but in the end it did not materialize. The burdened brother again penned the prayer that God would 'reveal himSelf in his Son to their Souls'. In 1776, he heard that Eunice was still alive and 'in Health' – he prayed again that God might reveal himself to her 'that she may be Saved in the day of the Lord'. In his last prayer for Eunice composed in 1778, the ageing brother again evoked the childhood trauma shared with his sister. He received a report from one who had seen her that she was well: 'I am glad to hear from my sister who is in health and comfortably provided for . . . and pray to God to reveal himself in a Saving manner to her soul – notwithstanding the disadvantages she is under by a Superstitious Education.' With this final intercession, Williams brought to mind the influence of the Jesuits at Kahnawake, the mission near Montreal to which Eunice had been brought seven decades prior as a child captive. Her brother believed it was their false teaching that continued to cloud her judgement, impeding her embrace of spiritual truth. Thus Williams employed prayer as a prism through which to lament the lasting implications of the Deerfield raid, a violent episode which he believed had torn the Williams children not only from each other, but from the right understanding of God himself.[14]

While Williams's use of ejaculatory and intercessory prayer reflected common practices of his time, the third type of prayer in his diary, which I call narrative prayer, was a practice devised to suit his own spiritual needs. In this particular strand of supplication, Williams gave mundane matters transcendent meaning by assigning them spiritual significance. Prompted by events of daily life, he began his diary entry with a simple observation and concluded it with an appeal to eternal principles. Narrative prayer was yet another means by which Williams was able to sustain his accountability to God for the days given to him since his childhood preservation. In a typical example of a narrative prayer penned by Williams in 1735, the minister linked the paying of his salary to the prospect of his mortality: 'This day the people are bringing in their rates. The Lord be pleased to give me to realize the great & awfull day of accounts that I must be brought unto.' In early 1741, at the age of forty-seven, he had been contemplating the proper disposition of his worldly estate: 'I have been new drafting my will. The Lord give me to realize – my dissolution & prepare me for it.' A day after taking care of this rather sobering business, the pastor expressed a more hopeful outlook on his spiritual destiny: 'This day I went to the Singing Lecture in the West – parish . . . the Lord prepare me – to Sing with him Eternally.' He ended the month of January 1741 with a prayer we might expect from a New England minister in the winter: 'a very Stormy Season – blessed be God – for the comfortable accommodations we have'. In thousands of narrative prayers such as these, composed over a lifetime, Williams aimed to find the sacred in the everyday.[15]

In a particular type of narrative prayer dedicated to the memory of the Deerfield raid, Williams used the anniversary of the raid as a prompt to recall God's actions in the past and ask that he remember their significance in the present. On 28 February 1730, he described the attack on his childhood home as follows: 'This day 26 years ago I was captivated by the Indians – the Lord be pleased to affect me with his Frowns & mercies.' Although brief, these remarks bore characteristic features that recurred in his Deerfield-related diary entries: he acknowledged the number of years it had been since the raid, he described his capture – in this case, he was 'captivated' (other times he was 'taken prisoner' or 'carried away to Canada') and he indicated the active role of God in this life since that day. On the twenty-eighth anniversary of the Deerfield attack in 1732, Williams observed in his diary:

> Oh the trouble & distress I and my Father's family & our neighbours were – therein . . . but oh the mercies & kindness of the Lord our God to us to me in Speciall who was remarkably preserved & kept alive – & God has mercifully brought me along hitherto & has given me a family and many family comforts & blessings.

Two decades later in 1752, Williams recounted these events again: 'This day 48 years ago I was taken captive by the Indians – a memorable day. How God has been waiting upon me these 48 years – I praise him for his great Goodness and desire to be humbled – for my own baseness and ingratitude.' In 1779, at the age of eighty-six, Williams was still offering prayers in remembrance of his childhood preservation: 'This is a memorable day', he began his prayerful reflection,

> tis Seventy-five years Since I was taken captive by the Indians – God has done Great things for me – waited a long time upon me, & has

been very Gracious to me – I praise & thank him – would call upon my Soul & all within me to bless his name.

The theme of God's patience in waiting for Williams to live into the fullness of the blessing of his preservation is the thread that connects these commemorative prayers together over time. It speaks to Williams's abiding sense of his inability to live up to the promise of God's mercy in sparing his life.[16]

The final mode of prayer in Williams's diary is that of preparatory prayer. Every eight weeks, the congregation at Longmeadow celebrated the Lord's Supper. On the eve of this celebration, which Williams called the 'Sabbath and Sacrament', the pastor composed an elaborate prayer in his diary which articulated his needs and those of his flock. Formal in tone and design, these prayers were grounded in a spirit of penance and written in a manner that allowed Williams to engage in private piety before most likely offering these prayers publicly before his flock the next day.

Williams always anticipated his approach of the Lord's Table with an impassioned declaration of his unworthiness. These opening lines from a 1722 preparatory prayer capture the spirit of his approach: 'I bewail before God, my Stupidness, my Senselessness, my Great dullness in duties of religion, my very Great concernedness about the world.' Once he framed his prayer accordingly, Williams gave thanks for the blessings he and those around him had known 'since the last Sacrament' and he offered intercessions for his family, flock and region. He noted in one such prayer in 1730: 'I desire oh Lord to give up my Family, my children Particularly unto Thee.' In 1762, he gave thanks that his daughter was safely delivered of a child: 'She is now, so well as to be here this day, with her Son – oh that God's goodness might Suitably affect me.' In one of the last Sabbath and Sacrament prayers he crafted before his death in 1782, he appealed to the familiar theme of desiring God's favour for his congregation: 'Oh Lord be pleased to bless this flock . . . be pleased to pour out thy Spirit upon this people and don't leave and forsake them.'[17]

Williams also used these prayers to remember the world beyond Longmeadow, praying in 1748 for the concerns of England as well as those of New England: 'I pray God to bless our nation, to advance his own interest, & Kingdom in the world. Be pleased to bless this Land – in all its interest.' Williams echoed this theme in 1762: 'Be pleased to bless this place, this Town, this Land, our Nation, all the British dominions, and take care of Zion.' This theme was a constant in his Sabbatarian prayers, surfacing again toward the end of his life in 1780: 'The Lord be pleased to pity, pardon, reform, & help & protect this Land.'[18]

As Williams's preparatory prayers concluded, he found himself alone again before the Table of God. Williams concluded these prayers with the request that God be with him at the Sacrament the next day and he did so in a variety of ways. In 1730, he summoned the vision of a heavenly meal: 'Graciously meet with me at thy table, & oh Lord, and be pleased to prepare me to eat bread & drink wine with thee, in thy Heavenly Kingdom.' In 1733, he invoked a hoped-for glimpse of the holy: 'Oh Lord for a Sight of Christ at his table – that I might see him to be lovely.' There is tenderness in his intention from the winter of 1741: 'Oh Lord – graciously meet with me with a Father's blessing, at thy table.' While Williams found many ways to ask for this blessing, the underlying hope was the same: that he might find spiritual reassurance at the Table of God.[19]

On occasion the memories of the Deerfield attack found their way into the prayers Williams crafted in anticipation of the Sabbath and Sacrament. Again we see him using his diary as a site for the prayerful consideration of the trauma he endured as a child. If the anniversary of the raid fell near the celebration of the Lord's Supper every two months, Williams might revisit a commemorative entry through the lens of preparatory prayer. As noted above, Williams remembered the Deerfield anniversary on 28 February 1752 by noting that God was 'still waiting' on him. In his prayer anticipating the Sacrament of 1 March 1752 that followed in his diary, Williams forged a direct link between his childhood experiences and his ever-present sense of unworthiness. He opened with praise for God, who was willing to 'condescend to take notice of poor sinners', chief among them Williams himself. He then proceeded to narrate his experiences of nearly fifty years prior: '[It has been] 48 years since I was taken prisoner – I was carried to Canada – preserved and returned – and have received remarkable favours from God. I would be humbled before God for my sin, baseness, and ingratitude – my incorrigibleness under judgments.' Thus, in the voice of prayer, Williams retold the tale of his childhood and linked those experiences to his adult life, folding his trials into the larger narrative of God's mercy and his own sinfulness.[20]

The same pattern emerged about fifteen years later in a series of Williams's diary entries in 1768. On 3 March 1768 Williams described offering a sermon at a meeting of some in his congregation before the Sacrament. Likely inspired by the anniversary of the Deerfield raid, he reflected upon the events of his childhood in his message to those gathered: 'I took notice of the destruction of the providence of God in the destruction of Deerfield 64 years ago and of the providence of God towards me and towards this place.' Two days later on the eve of the Sacrament of 5 March 1768, Williams again narrated the events of his childhood:

> I desire to bear on my mind the divine rebuke of Providence in the destruction of my Native town ... I would also call to mind the great goodness of God to me and my friends that I was remarkably preserved and returned ... oh how a long time God has been waiting upon me – been trying and proving me.

Again we see the theme of God's intervention on Williams's behalf as a child and his patient shaping of Williams's character ever since. Thus, not only did Williams uphold the importance of these childhood events in the practice of his own piety – recounting them faithfully in his diary – he held out the remembrance of them to his Longmeadow congregation decades later as a reminder that God had shown mercy on him as a child and that he was always at work shaping the intricate details of human affairs.[21]

As a written compendium of prayer in eighteenth-century New England, the Stephen Williams diary is a remarkable source as to the disciplined pursuit of this pious practice across a lifetime. In appealing to God through ejaculatory, intercessory, narrative and preparatory prayers, Williams spent decades remembering and reflecting upon the traumatic events of his childhood. Framed by the cross-cultural violence of the 1704 Deerfield raid, Williams looked to prayer as a means by which to shape his diary and express his accountability for the days he had been given since his childhood preservation. Prayer also offered Williams a means by which to seek relief from the sense of unworthiness that hung over him as one who had been spared 'in Special', even as God continued to 'wait upon him' over the years of his very long life.

Notes

[1] G. Sheldon, *A History of Deerfield, Massachusetts* . . ., vol. 1 (Greenfield, 1895-6); R. I. Melvoin, *New England Outpost: War and Society in Colonial Deerfield* (New York, 1989); J. Demos, *The Unredeemed Captive: A Family Story From Early America* (New York, 1995), pp. 1-39; J. Lepore, *The Name of War: King Philip's War and the Origin of American Identity* (New York, 1998), pp. 71-96; E. Haefeli and K. Sweeney, *Captors and Captives: The 1704 French and Indian Raid on Deerfield* (Amherst, 2003), pp. 1-142.

[2] Haefeli and Sweeney, *Captors and Captives*, pp. 113-15, 130, 137, 149, 169-171.

[3] In his narrative of captivity, 'What Befell Stephen Williams in his Captivity', Stephen Williams described the scene as follows: 'On the last [day] of February 1703/4 the French and Indians came and surprised our fort and took it. And after they had broken into our house and took us prisoners, they barbarously murdered a brother and sister as they did several of our neighbors'; in E. Haefeli and K. Sweeney (eds), *Captive Histories: English, French, and Native Narratives of the 1704 Deerfield Raid* (Amherst, 2006), p. 161. In his narrative, *The Redeemed Captive Retuning to Zion*, John Williams added the detail about the door: 'some were so cruel as to take and carry to the door two of my children and murder them'; in Haefeli and Sweeney (eds), *Captive Histories*, p. 96.

[4] Stephen's account of Eunice Mather's death is found in 'What Befell Stephen Williams', in Haefeli and Sweeney (eds), *Captive Histories*, p. 162. John Williams's account is found in *The Redeemed Captive*, in Haefeli and Sweeney (eds), *Captive Histories*, pp. 99-100.

[5] Stephen Williams, 'What Befell Stephen Williams', in Haefeli and Sweeney (eds), *Captive Histories*, p. 166.

[6] On early almanacs, see M. McCarthy, *The Accidental Diarist: A History of the Daily Planner in America* (Chicago, 2013), pp. 11-53; M. Barber Stowell, *Early American Almanacs: The Colonial Weekday Bible* (New York, 1977); B. S. Capp, *English Almanacs, 1500-1800: Astrology and the Popular Press* (Ithaca, 1979); and D. D. Hall, *Worlds of Wonder, Days of Judgement: Popular Religious Belief in Early New England* (Cambridge, 1990), pp. 58-61. On prayer in early New England, see C. Hambrick-Stowe, *The Practice of Piety: Puritan Devotional Disciplines in Seventeenth-Century New England* (Chapel Hill, 1982), pp. 175-86; Hall, *Worlds of Wonder*, pp. 121, 145, 166, 199-204, 231-4, 236; and R. Naeher, 'Prayerful Voice: Self-Shaping, Intimacy, and the Puritan Practice and Experience of Prayer', University of Connecticut PhD thesis, 1999.

[7] Hambrick-Stowe, *Practice of Piety*, pp. 185-6.

[8] Diary I: 82, 28 September 1717. The Stephen Williams diary exists in multiple forms. The manuscript diaries are stored by the First Church of Christ, Longmeadow, Massachusetts, in a local bank deposit box and are not accessible to the public. Microfilm images of the manuscript diary are available electronically on the website of the Storrs Memorial Library in Longmeadow, Massachusetts. The Works Progress Administration (WPA) transcription of the Williams diary made in the 1930s is available in hard copy at the Storrs Library and in digital form at the library's website. All diary entries quoted here have been checked against digital images of the manuscript diaries. In citing the diary, I have used the volume number and page number as they appear in the WPA version. I have retained original spelling, punctuation and capitalization when possible, but have expanded contracted words. I have also converted dashes and the abbreviation '&c.' at the ends of sentences to periods. All dates appear as if the New Year begins on 1 January, not 25 March. All quotations from the Bible are from the King James Version.

9   Diary I: 152, 29 September 1718; I: 210, 17 June 1719.
10 Diary I: 271, 2 February 1721; II: 29, 20 September 1728; I: 360, 11 June 1722; II: 196, 31 July 1730; II: 352, 15 June 1733; III: 136, 14 March 1737.
11 Diary IV: 14, 15 October 1756; VI: 17, 7 September 1762; VI: 149, 5 July 1764; IX: 334, 1 May 1778.
12 Diary III: 382–4, 20–27 July 1741.
13 Diary V: 345–8, 30 June–10 July 1761.
14 Diary VI: 256, 21 November 1765; VI: 369, 20 February 1767; VIII: 230, 21 December 1773; IX: 359, 10 July 1778.
15 Diary III: 7, 24 February 1735; III: 346–9, 13–29 January 1741.
16 Diary II: 172, 28 February 1730; II: 278, 29 February 1732; IV: 182, 29 February 1752; X: 23, 11 March 1779. (The date change for the anniversary in 1779 was due to the conversion from the Julian to Gregorian calendar in 1752.)
17 Diary I: 330, 6 January 1722; II: 181, 2 May 1730; VI: 1–2, 3 July 1762; X: 295, 3 November 1781.
18 Diary IV: 70, 25 June 1748; VI: 2, 3 July 1762; X: 147, 6 May 1780.
19 Diary II: 203, 19 September 1730; II: 323, 6 January 1733; III: 345, 3 January 1741.
20 Diary IV: 182–3, 28 February 1752.
21 Diary VII: 53–6, 3–5 March 1768.

THE EYE OF A NEEDLE: COMMEMORATING THE 'GODLY MERCHANT' IN THE EARLY MODERN FUNERAL SERMON

Penny Pritchard

This investigation contributes to a much larger ongoing study of the early modern Protestant funeral sermon which considers the genre's origins and its surprising popularity during print culture's rapid expansion. Subjects for these works range from anonymous infants to the nation's monarch, as well as a host of 'ordinary' individuals often characterized, on the text's title page, by their profession.[1] While approximately half of several thousand extant funeral sermons from this period commemorate deceased ministers and their wives, a significant proportion acknowledge other professions, most notably doctors, the military, and merchants.[2]

This last cohort presents particular challenges for ministers seeking to endorse the spiritual conduct of those whose earthly success is defined by material profit. This article's title alludes to Matthew 19:24, the scriptural text most frequently associated with the difficulty of salvation faced by men who possess material wealth ('And again I say unto you, It is easier for a camel to go through the eye of a needle, than for a rich man to enter into the kingdom of God'). The full meaning of this text, however, encompassing the passage through to Matthew 19:26, relates to God's infinite capacity to achieve what is otherwise impossible, and thus implicitly guarantees at least the potential of salvation for those possessing earthly riches.[3] By this principle, at least, the soteriological concerns of England's Protestant merchants appear to be hampered less by biblical doctrine than by increased cultural scrutiny of their moral conduct during the early modern period. There is no doubt that truly profound questions about how the acquisition of wealth might be reconciled with spiritual content in Protestant early modern England, most famously posed by Max Weber more than a century ago, become a more urgent cultural concern in the wake of growing mercantile activity. Such questions continue to shape our understanding of the history and also the literary culture of this period, though they remain subject to scholarly debate beyond the remit of this discussion.[4] That said, the opening of Weber's important fifth chapter, 'Asceticism and the Spirit of Capitalism', usefully stresses the influence of both clergy and (theological) texts, as well as associated cultural practices and rituals, on the social construction of the English national character:

> In order to comprehend the connection between the basic religious ideas of ascetic Protestantism and the maxims of everyday economic life, it is necessary above all to draw upon those theological texts that can be recognized as having crystallized out of the practice of pastoral care. In this [sixteenth- and seventeenth-century] epoch, everything depended upon admission to the sacrament of communion. Moreover, through pastoral care, church discipline, and preaching, the clergy's influence grew to such an extent – as any glance in the collected *consillia, casus conscientiae*, and other documents will indicate – that we today are *simply no longer* capable of understanding its broad scope. Religious forces, as they became transmitted to populations through *these regular practices* and became legitimate and accepted, were decisive for the formation of 'national character'.[5]

It is with acknowledgement of this powerful, if cautiously broad, textual influence – as well as the Weberian concept of 'elective affinity', as usefully defined and endorsed by Patrick Collinson, among others – that I justify my approach here in interpreting interactions between prevailing religious beliefs in early modern England and contemporary social activities, such as the impact of print culture, through popular religious writing.[6] This investigation therefore makes a tacit assumption that selective cross-influences may be recognized across the Protestant faith(s) of the minister-authors whose works are considered here, and their conscious participation in contemporary print culture – in its broadest sense – as discernible in published funeral sermons. The cultural status of the early modern merchant, though subject to substantial scholarly consideration for some time, merits further juxtaposition against the contemporary context of an increasingly self-regarding print culture whose ascendance paralleled the period's economic expansion on both a European and global scale, and with it, a growing social category of merchants and other capitalists actively engaged in its pursuit.

One justification for this investigation's consideration of a hitherto relatively neglected genre of popular religious print, then, is to determine whether evidence from published funeral sermons reinforces or remains distinct from what other contemporary forms of print describe concerning what I will call 'mercantile conduct'. This is intended to refer to print descriptions of the moral, spiritual and (where relevant) commercial behaviour of men engaged in mercantile trade throughout the latter seventeenth- and eighteenth-century period, both in terms of fictional and 'authentic' portraits. No comparative distinction will be made, here, between Protestant sects or denominations, given the very broad array of doctrinal and sectarian positions upheld both within and outside of the established Church throughout this period. Economic factors which categorize merchants, such as 'wealth' or sectors of trading activity, are also less of a concern here than more universal principles of mercantile conduct, such as moral integrity or diligence. This notwithstanding, it should be acknowledged, as Ralph Houlbrooke has observed concerning the preaching of early modern funeral sermons, that such public services of commemoration 'usually had to be paid for. Most of the poor probably went to their graves without them.'[7] It is more than likely that the extant funeral sermons considered here, possessing too the further distinction of publication, commemorate merchants who experienced no small degree of material success in their lifetimes.[8]

In blurring the religious or economic subcategories between Protestant merchants commemorated in published funeral sermons, the main intention is to consider how contemporary descriptions of early modern mercantile conduct in print – even if they tell us very little about individual merchants – help us to understand what sort of cultural expectations were associated with the figure of the 'godly merchant' in early modern England at the time when popular print culture began to play an increasingly important role in shaping those expectations. England's rapid economic expansion, with London overtaking Amsterdam as the commercial centre of Europe by the early eighteenth century, provides some justification for increased cultural scrutiny of mercantile conduct in this period.[9] A significant proportion of the literary record further supports the biblical claim, made above, that mercantile conduct can be wholly compatible with Christian virtues – in particular, through diligence, regular habits, abstention and generous philanthropy. In conduct works such as *Character and Qualification of an Honest Loyal Merchant* (1686) or *A Letter from an Old Merchant to his Son* (1753), or as demonstrated in the very letter and example of *Family-Prayers and Moral Essays in Prose and Verse, by a Merchant* (1769), the uncomplicated marriage of Christian and mercantile interests is readily apparent.

A clear delineation needs to be made between those literary works of the late seventeenth century which praise, sometimes unquestioningly, the endeavours of an emerging mercantile class and works which interrogate specifically Christian virtues most readily associated with those endeavours. The previous category is often recognized in relation to prominent Royal Society members whose agenda encompassed mercantile endeavour in relation to a much wider 'project' of social reform. John Evelyn's celebration of merchants, for example, represents just one element of his and others' much larger social project which, as John McVeagh points out, is

> packed with descriptions and experiments, improvements, discoveries, mercantile activities, commercial projects, scientific pursuits, speculative attempts on the difficult or impossible for their own sake and for the good they may produce. All of these forms of endeavour are combined together as if Evelyn recognizes no basic difference between them; and this is indeed the case, for the spirit informing the personal record is purely Baconian[.][10]

Some clear parallels exist between the Baconian recognition of mercantile endeavour and the 'godly merchant' to be investigated here. However, a useful contrast may be demonstrated by considering the relative insignificance of religious conduct in the former example versus the exemplary Christian conduct of Solomon, as definitively asserted in Defoe's *Complete English Tradesman* of 1726, when he observes that King Solomon was

> certainly a friend to men of business, as it appears by his frequent good advice to them. In *Proverbs Chapter 18, verse 9*, he says, 'He that is slothful in business, is brother to him that is a great waster:' and in another place, 'The sluggard shall be clothed in rags,' (*Proverbs 22, verse 1*) ... the same wise man, by way of encouragement, tells them, 'The diligent hand maketh rich,' (*Proverbs 10, verse 4*), and, 'The diligent shall bear rule, but the slothful shall be under tribute.'[11]

Here, Defoe's moral equation of diligent 'men of business' with godly followers of Solomon's 'good advice' illustrates a wholly unproblematic depiction of the Protestant work ethic.[12] A much earlier Solomonic parallel, endorsing idealized mercantile conduct, may be found in *Character and Qualification of an Honest Loyal Merchant* (1686), which defends not only the honourable status of the merchant as a role befitting even those of noble birth, but also seeks to describe Solomon's identity in terms which unite the economic activities and even geographical locations of mercantilism in biblical and contemporary times:

> The Truth is, the wisest of Kings and Men has long since given his Judgement by his practice in this case; for Solomon himself could never have made Silver and Gold to be as plenteous in Jerusalem as Stones, and Cedars as Sycamores, if he had not first turned Merchant, join'd in Copartnership with King Hiram, and set out a Navy at Ezion Geher (a Port in the Red Sea) which had the Advantage of Traffic to the Indian Ocean, and from thence to Ophir (supposed to be the Isle of Madagascar) whence they brought Gold and Silver and Elephants Teeth, as well as Apes and Peacocks.[13]

Solomon's precedent anticipates the successful and 'godly' merchant who happily resolves the moral challenges presented by the twin endeavours of capitalism and Christianity. Yet while the anonymous author of *Character and Qualification of an Honest Merchant* might share Defoe's Solomonic parallel, his agenda is neither precisely the same as that of Defoe's later conduct work, nor does it echo wholly those Royal Society projectors (such as John Evelyn or Thomas Sprat) who celebrate more widely the 'Baconian endeavours' of the age. In the first case, the author of *Character and Qualification* is more volubly defensive in tone than Defoe's later *Complete English Tradesmen* in championing the social status and 'Noble Mystery' of trade:

> I intend [. . .] to vindicate the Honour of Merchandize, and convince the World, That if a Person of Quality should happen to breed up his Son, or Match a Daughter therein, there's no danger that they should presently be level'd with the common Crowd, or Numbred with the Gaffers and the Gamers. [. . .]
>
> SURE I am, whatever low Conceits Aristotle or some other Pedants may have had of Merchandize in old times, when its

Dignity was not known, and when indeed it was but Huckstering and Pedlary in respect of what it has since arriv'd to; it must be avow'd, That 'tis long since become not unworthy of Persons of first Quality [. . .]

TO go higher, some of the most sacred Crowned Heads of Christendom, descended from, and ally'd to the most Ancient and Illustrious Families that the World can boast of; (and in that number principally our present most August and Gracious Sovereign), are so far from connting [sic] it any diminution to their Royal Majesties, That in the highest manner they endeavour to encourage Trade, by interesting Themselves therein.[14]

In the second case, the author of *Character and Qualification* also places his own views on the glories of trade in perspective to the earlier, though more recent, example of Royal Society discourses by quoting at length – while mildly expressing his own detachment from – a 1680 pamphlet which scorns the Baconian projectors with near-Swiftian relish:

'Tis a smart, but I hope, causeless Reflection of a late Ingenious (*) Author. 'We are (says he) still pretending to be more Acurate in Logick and Philosophy (which however otherwise useful, do not add Twopence per Annum to the Riches of the Nation) we continue to squeeze all the Sapless Papers and Fragments of Antiquity; we grow mighty well acquainted with the old Heathen gods, Towns, and People; we prise [sic] our selves in fruitless curiosities; we turn our Lice and Fleas into Bulls and Pigs by our Magnifying Glasses; we are searching for the world in the Moon with our Telescopes; we send to weight the Air on the top of Teneriff; we invent Paceing Saddles, and Gimcracks of all sorts, which are voted Ingenuities, whilst the solid and most useful Notions and Considerations of Trade, are turned into a Ridicule, or out of Fashion.[']'[15]

Though the author of *Character and Qualification* does make a modest effort to preface this lengthy extract with his hope that such observations are 'causeless', it is less clear whether, in doing so, he seeks to distance himself from its mockery of 'fruitless curiosities' and 'Gimcracks' of scientific invention, or from its expression of vexed frustration that contemporary ridicule is being levelled at trade, or both. Whatever the case, his position is not identical to that of the Royal Society, and is instead far more dedicated to an idealisation of the figure of the merchant himself as both godly and prosperous, and wholly reconciled in these features. Such figures remain more culturally familiar in idealized and fictional forms than in contemporary extant accounts of 'authentic' godly merchants whose lives are self-documented. As Matthew Kadane observes in the 2013 introduction to his exploration of the spiritual diary of prosperous Leeds cloth merchant Joseph Ryder,

> [w]e still know less than we should, however, about the birth pangs of modern capitalism felt by the pious people whose commerce and labor brought it about. In a history rich with images of titans and victims of the market, and celebrants and skeptics of consumerism, the obscure figure is the godly entrepreneur on the cusp of industrialization, wrestling with the moral meaning of unknown economic opportunity.[16]

The scope to research the lived experience of tradesmen such as Joseph Ryder through their spiritual diaries remains challenging for many reasons (as Kadane outlines), not least of which are the cultural currency of autobiographical writing in this period and – in tandem with this – the extent to which such forms of writing present the subject as unique yet, at the same time, an everyman suited to strategic cultural analysis.[17] Notwithstanding these challenges, as well as some very important scholarly discussions surrounding the extent to which such diaries were intended both for posterity and the writer's private reflection, spiritual autobiographies and diaries necessarily offer the reader a self-fashioned portrait of a living subject.[18] The published funeral sermon, then, sits squarely between these genres of literary idealization and spiritual autobiography; it commemorates an authentic subject externally depicted but competes, in the early modern period, for a readership whose taste for popular religious literature may well have encompassed all of these categories and may not have necessarily distinguished readily between fictional versus non-fictional versions of the merchants they encountered there.

As such, this investigation suggests an alternative and problematized cultural portrait of the early modern 'godly merchant' which also looks to literary precedents for comparative analysis. The literary record is profoundly ambivalent. Despite extensive acknowledgement of Defoe's and other positive examples in the early decades of the eighteenth century, John McVeagh has summarized the post-Restoration literary portrait of the merchant, particularly in terms of drama, as both largely negative and indifferent. This can be seen not only in the 'comic rather than menacing aspects of those such as vulgar tradesmen', but also in the calculated materialism of Wycherley's merchants. It is only Dryden, notes McVeagh, who offers an 'altogether more complicated response to the whole issue of capitalist growth', and though still largely a negative one, he

> could at times share in the mercantile ebullience which he also criticised in its grosser aspect, and well represents in his variations of theme and emphasis over forty years, despite his lack of enthusiasm for what it was becoming, a shifting society striking out for itself new necessary valuations all the time. Perhaps for Dryden the old ones were being let too casually slip out of respect; but he is engaged with, not withdrawn from a nation not yet settled into that commercialized, acquisitive, imperialist role which was to be its character for the ensuing two and a half centuries and more.[19]

If the post-Restoration merchant in drama represents a largely nostalgic and gloomy Tory outlook on the imminent arrival of that 'commercialized, acquisitive, imperialist' national role, much less frequently are 'real' merchants openly castigated in print for either moral or religious misconduct in the period contemporary with all the works in this estimation considered by McVeagh. Theatrical portraits are clearly not the same as commemorative representations of deceased people, notwithstanding the fluid nature of boundaries between different textual genres in the early modern period. Nevertheless, an equally if different type of ambiguity is discernible in merchants' funeral sermons, though as often as not this results from what has been omitted from the commemorative portrait of the deceased merchant. The real possibility of cross-influence from literary examples of merchants is unsurprising, given the fact that published funeral sermons competed with many other types of literature for popular recognition from a burgeoning readership who invested rather less in distinguishing between genres than they did in discerning useful didactic content from them. In early works of prose fiction, such as Defoe's *Robinson Crusoe* or *The Family Instructor*, the didactic value of such writing is unquestionably part of how they are presented to the reading public. As much is apparent in the manner of which such texts were prefaced:

> we live in an age that does not want so much to know their duty as to practice it; not so much to be taught, as to be made obedient to what they have already learnt ... The way I have taken for this, is entirely New, and at first perhaps it may appear something Odd, and the Method may be contemned; But let such blame their own more irregular Tempers, that must have every thing turned into new Models; must be touch'd with Novelty, and have their Fancies humour'd with the Dress of a Thing; so that if it be what has been said over and over a thousand times, yet if it has but a different colour'd Coat, or a new Feather in its Cap, it pleases and wins upon them, whereas the same Truths written in the divinest Stile in the World, would be flat, stale and unpleasant without it.[20]

The cultural influence of the published funeral sermon was on the wane by the time that later works of extended prose fiction began to assume their popular ascendance as 'novels'. Carol Stewart has even gone so far as to suggest that 'the idea particular novels, if not the novel as a genre, could promote morality in a way that sermons failed to do was beginning to take hold in the mid-eighteenth century', but even if this is the case, the strongly comparative nature of her observation points to the cultural overlap between sermonic literature (including published funeral sermons) and the growing moral influence of didactic works of prose fiction in tandem with their growing popularity.[21] It can come as no surprise that readers and congregations would likewise carry their tastes for 'entertaining' as well as 'improving' content to their reading of contemporary funeral sermons, particularly as they concern the matter of depicting the deceased's moral and spiritual integrity. Ralph Houlbrooke asserts as much, noting also the implicit challenges this scrutiny posed for the presiding minister:

> The last part of the [funeral] sermon, in which it was customary to describe the character of the dead person, was awaited with the keenest anticipation. The preacher's task was clearly a delicate one. But by carefully selecting what was good from the life's record, and drawing a veil over the rest, he might usually satisfy the expectations of his audience without violating his own conscience. In many

cases, clergy went further, emphasising the grounds for hope of a happy outcome, or even expressing confidence that the deceased had entered a better world.²²

Houlbrooke's reference to how ministers attempted to strike a balance between 'what was good from the life's record, and drawing a veil over the rest' offers one aspect of how such ministers convey mercantile conduct in contemporary funeral sermons. In short, they attempt to offer a proportional balance of merchants' active versus passive Christian virtues. Active virtues include hard work, an enquiring mind, and brotherly love as exemplified through charitable acts or work in the community. In 1753, the Old Merchant exhorts his son to active pursuit of knowledge through the study of a wide spectrum of improving literature, both secular and spiritual:

> Read History and natural Philosophy at your leisure Hours, that you may know GOD and Man by their Works. Read the Old *Whole Duty of Man*, that you may know, and govern yourself. Above all read the Scriptures . . . Read the Prophet Isaiah, and compare him with the History of Christ, that you may see the Conformity between the divine Foreknowledge and the Facts in which we are so deeply concerned [. . .] Read the Psalms that your Heart may be warmed with true Devotion . . . Let the New Testament be ever in your Hands, that you may know, and well consider, on what Terms Salvation is promised.²³

This advice is preceded, however, with plentiful admonitions to the Old Merchant's son to refrain from sinful practices and company, thus tempering active virtues with those of passive abstinence:

> When you go into Company, be not assuming; be not first to give your Opinion, nor positive . . . Let not the Atheist, the Deist, or the Libertine, whether in Principle or Practice, be among your Intimates. If sometimes you are obliged to meet them over a Bottle, guard against that and them, with a like Abhorrence to Intoxication.²⁴

Nearly seventy years prior to the publication of the *Letter from an Old Merchant to his Son*, the author of *Character and Qualification of an Honest Loyal Merchant* had celebrated in no uncertain terms the merchant's active, indeed Providential, virtues as a missionary and global peacemaker:

> Without [the Merchant] the world would still be a kind of Wilderness, one part unknown and unbeholding to the other; and if ever its remote Inhabitants met, it would be rather for mischief or slaughter . . . whereas his part unites divided Empires, and those that never beheld the same Stars; joins people separated by different Climates, Religions, and Policies, into one common Society . . . Nay, further, there seems yet a more sublime and mysterious designment of Providence attending his pains; for by establishing an intercourse with Infidels for Civil Traffick, a door is not seldom open'd to advance the Divine Interest; so that he may propagate our most Holy Faith, as well as end our Temporal Commodities[.][25]

Yet even this dynamic and godly figure of mercantile agency also encompasses the accompanying passive virtue of honesty, since the virtuous Merchant would also

> rather endure the Rack himself, than stretch a Piece of Cloath on the Tenters to make it three or four Yards longer, which then sold to a Turk, shall in the next Shower, Cockle all up in a Ruck causing the honest *Musulman* to revile both the cheating Christian and his Religion[.][26]

This idealized balance of active and passive Christian mercantile virtues is not merely a literary motif; Perry Gauci describes a similar balance in 'the common code of conduct' for City of London merchants in the international context, when he observes that

> the [mercantile] profession had historically promoted personal values which reflected the priorities of the business world. If any common code of conduct was maintained within trading circles, it centred on the virtues of industry, reliability, punctuality, thrift and good faith . . . advised for many other walks of life, . . . they gained a particular significance when so much of international business hinged on the maintenance of trust. Private records suggest that within the City [of London] these attributes were not taken lightly, and any loss of respect on these grounds, whether

by the trader himself or any of his circle, spelt serious difficulty for the business.[27]

Balancing active and passive Christian virtues had long been discerned by City merchants as pragmatic, representing what Gauci goes on to describe as 'a general code of business behaviour vital to both individual and collective success . . . [since] the inherent self-interest in the maintenance of these basic principles of good conduct . . . in turn instilled a common outlook to the dealing world as a whole'.[28] The moral reconciliation of mercantile conduct with Christian virtue appears eminently possible, it seems, as reflected by the (secular) historical record.

Given this array of textual portraits of the early modern merchant – whether castigated by Wycherley, celebrated by Waller and Defoe, or idealized as possessing a balance of passive and active virtues in works of moral and religious instruction – and reinforced by Gauci's evidence of the pragmatic interests of actual merchants in this period – readers might reasonably expect something similar in merchants' contemporary funeral sermons. They would be disappointed on several fronts. Conspicuous by their absence, extraordinarily few published funeral sermons openly commemorate merchants as their subject during the early modern period.[29] This is not to suggest that merchants rarely received funeral sermons. Either very few published examples survive (though this seems unlikely, given the significant extant presence of other professions mentioned on funeral sermons' title pages) or, alternatively, the mercantile identity of the deceased was rarely openly promoted.

The same chronological period covered by this investigation witnesses, comparatively, as least as many, if not more, published funeral sermons for merchants' wives. These include Thomas Brooks's highly popular and oft-reprinted *A String of Pearls*, a funeral sermon ostensibly commemorating Mary Blake, printed in least ten separate editions between 1657 and 1684, as well as Joseph Hill's *The Providence of God in Sudden Death* (a funeral sermon for Mary Reve) published in Rotterdam in 1685, Edmund Batson's 1700 funeral sermon for Mary Paice, and Boston minister Charles Chauncy's funeral sermon for Lucy Waldo in 1741.[30] Published funeral sermons for the most successful English merchants are in truth very rare, even in the case of merchants notable for public activities beyond trade. Neither Daniel Colwall, for example, founder and early bankroller of the Royal Society, nor Sir Dalby Thomas, colonial merchant and prolific author as well as commissioner for the Million Act and Malt Act Lotteries (Thomas was also the recipient of Defoe's dedication of his *Essay Upon Projects* in 1697), has a funeral sermon extant.[31] The same applies to Sir Joseph Herne, East India Company governor, parliamentary minister and generous benefactor to Dartmouth, who paid for his own 'sumptuous funeral' in 1699 and 'substantial vault' at St Stephens, Coleman Street, where he also commissioned a wax effigy by the same artist who designed Queen Mary's.[32]

This apparent lack of formal commemoration in published funeral sermons seems even more surprising when we consider how many successful merchants were also generous benefactors and philanthropists who played an active role in their religious communities, both within and outside the established Church. David Hancock's *Citizens of the World* considers in detail the many large-scale philanthropic projects undertaken by four affluent London merchants in the second half of the eighteenth century (none of whom have published funeral sermons), while Perry Gauci further observes how early modern mercantile activity within the religious community forms just part of the wider array of international networks – religious and philanthropic, political, and even scientific – in which it was in merchants' best business interests to sustain an active profile :

> Religious belief and practice helped to solidify these networks of family and friends. [...] Given their wealth and status, merchants were usually assured a prominent place within these spiritual communities, which in turn could help breed mutual respect and affability within their social and business circles. Quaker records suggest that their monthly meetings could arbitrate in disputes, or even stand for the reputation of members across the Atlantic. [...] Many merchants held lay offices, acting as churchwardens or elders of their respective churches, thereby formalizing their leadership of particular communities within the eastern City. The Church of England had increasing difficulty in coaxing overseas traders to undertake more minor offices, but a strong mercantile presence remained on the vestries of the eastern parishes.[33]

Given the breadth of public and philanthropic activity in which merchants took part, what are we to make of the paucity of their published funeral sermons? One reason might be the overarching challenges faced by minister-authors who, in the very act of publishing funeral sermons, left themselves perennially vulnerable to accusations of mercenary conduct. This is summarized in Defoe's own satirical *Hymn to the Funeral Sermon*, in which he remarks how 'Pulpit-Praises may be had / According as the Man of God is paid'.[34] More caustic still, in *The Hazard of a Death-Bed Repentance*, John Dunton warns 'the Birth and Quality of such Men does demand our Tribute of Respect and Veneration when they live ... [but] those Ministers that Preach their Funeral Sermons are yet less excusable than other Men, if they lessen or conceal their Whoredoms.'[35] While Dunton, here, refers specifically to the aristocracy rather than the mercantile elite, it is equally apparent that commemorating individuals whose earthly identity was inherently dedicated to profit-making would leave the presiding minister's 'Tribute of Respect and Veneration' doubly subject to such attacks. How, then, did ministers praise successful merchants in terms of their Christian virtues? From the handful of extant works, three merchants' funeral sermons can offer some comparative analysis with the contemporary portrait of the 'godly merchant' found elsewhere in the press. The primary focus throughout the remainder of this investigation considers how these sermons depict the character and virtues of the merchant, first, through scriptural texts selected for exegesis in the first section, and secondly in the smaller, later, section customarily dedicated to the deceased's biography and depiction of character.[36]

What is immediately striking is that all three ministers' selection of primary scriptural texts for exposition – as indicated on the sermons' title pages – emphasize not only wholly passive and submissive qualities of Christian conduct to be emulated by mourners and readers alike, but also in merchants' lives in general. Nathanael Waker selects Job 14:1 ('Man that is born of a woman, hath but a short time to live, and is full of trouble'); Presbyterian minister Timothy Rogers selects book I of Corinthians 8:3 ('For the Fashion of this World passeth away') and Benjamin Colman – in colonial Boston – selects Philippians 1:10 ('That ye may be sincere, and without offence till the day of Christ'). In this last example, emphasis of passive Christian virtue is achieved through further citation of two more texts on the title page.[37]

All three ministers go on to deploy some aspect of their deceased subjects' profession in their discourse, whether in metaphorical terms or otherwise. Waker offers an accounting analogy early on to demonstrate the paucity and ephemeral nature of man's earthly state: 'when we have adjusted all of his accounts, the total sum at the foot will amount to no more than a few broken figures, and a long row of Ciphers, which signifie nothing to his advantage, but only serve to augment his woes.'[38] Later, more epigrammatically, Waker reflects upon the speed with which death comes for the spiritually unprepared: 'he who has a great debt to pay at Easter thinks the Lent to be very short'.[39] Waker's intentions here, however, are not to imply mercenary characteristics in Lucas Lucie, his deceased subject; Lucie is vividly praised in the second section of the sermon, both in general Christian terms as a 'good Neighbour, and a faithful Friend, and a loving Master, and an Honest Man, and a steddy Christian', and as a virtuous Christian 'Merchant':

> [I]n relation to his Equals, and those with whom he had commerce (and they were not a few) he approv'd himself a Punctual and Just man ... He did not build his house upon the ruins of others, nor fill it when he had done with plunder'd goods; He did not drink the tears of Orphans, nor feast upon the grones of Widows ... he did not break Artificially to cheat his Creditors, and fill his own purse[.][40]

Waker's commemoration is almost wholly defined by Lucie's passive virtues – not cheating his creditors, not profiting by others' loss – as if to suggest that Waker was reluctant to elaborate on Lucie's more active mercantile virtues. This was not a minister who was likely to 'damn with faint praise'; elsewhere Waker is noticeably vociferous in making known his High Church views. His prefatory dedication of this sermon to Lucie's brother Jacob openly alludes to heated differences with certain members of his congregation, while his concluding pages roundly condemn the antimonarchists who – unlike the deceased subject – neglected, in 1644, the admonition in Hebrews 13:7 to 'obey them that have the rule over you, and submit yourselves', in favour of 'rapine and murder'.[41] Yet this same minister is notably cautious to praise his subject in terms associated with the active getting of earthly profit.

Waker is not alone in openly voicing his political alliances in a funeral sermon while sustaining a certain reluctance to elaborate on the active mercantile success, or even other active virtues, of his deceased subject. Twenty-eight years later, Presbyterian minister Timothy Rogers wastes no time in offering full-blooded praise to God and English seamen for valiant battle over the French (in June 1692) in his Epistle Dedicatory to the deceased's brother John:

And so we are now called by the late Victory that God gave our Fleet over the French at Sea; we adore him for inspiring our Admirals and our Seamen with Courage and Resolution, and for that eminent Success that he gave them in the day of Battle, wherein so many of our Enemies, and of their biggest Ships, sunk like Lead in the mighty Waters. And we hope, that as the Divine Providence has by this means began the Ruine of that great Enemy of Mankind, so it will entirely finish it[.][42]

These seem incongruously robust and political allusions, given his principal theme – the ephemeral nature of this world – in this funeral sermon for merchant Edmund Hill, who died very young (though notably successful) after a prolonged illness. Hill is not openly identified as a merchant on the title page, but the profession is implicit at several stages in the funeral sermon, as when Rogers dedicates the concluding section to other young persons, admonishing them with the image of those who die wealthy, but too soon to save their eternal souls:

Though their Lands are now called after their own Names, and though they gave Rise to those Families who flourish ... which their Industry and Money purchased ... indeed their Greatness and Riches could only procure a more pompous Funeral ... and a more costly place to lie in.[43]

Despite these admonitions concerning 'other' deceased wealthy men, Rogers depicts his particular subject in far more positive, though again largely passive, terms. Although Rogers does acknowledge some moments of mercantile bustle in Hill's past life (when he 'used to walk the Streets in a hurry after Business' and was 'active in his calling and managing of Trade and Business but a few months ago'), he also offers at length a threefold categorisation of Hill's Christian virtues, which underscore the deceased's passivity, meekness and patient resignation to his fate. These are comprised by his sweetness of temper, with pleasant conversation, affableness, meekness and sincerity; his being serviceable and charitable, 'though he was not forward to proclaim his charities', with 'no stingy narrow Soul'; and finally, submission in his long affliction, with great patience and resignation, taking – Rogers remarks – 'as much satisfaction on his sick-bed as in his warehouse, because it was the will of God'.[44]

The extent of Hill's resignation to his physical deterioration might seem incongruous in one so recently 'active in his calling and managing of Trade', but it is also a characteristic which Rogers finds particularly worthy of note, since he has already made allusion to it as early as the Epistle Dedicatory, when he remarks how 'It is therefore the Wisdom and the Love of God to his Servants, that he sends them various Afflictions, to wean them from so vain a state [. . .] his Wisdom that prepares the Cross, and his Love that teaches them to bear it.'[45] Patient submission to God's will is a Christian virtue worthy of emulation, but even more so in a twenty-four-year-old whose brief adult life had already witnessed material success. What both the commemorations by Rogers and Waker lack is any proportional recognition of the active Christian virtues found elsewhere in contemporary literary portraits of idealized merchants. This lack is highlighted differently, indeed problematically, by the third example to be considered here, the 1723 funeral sermon for David Stoddard (a Boston merchant who died at the age of thirty-seven), in which minister Benjamin Colman does initially acknowledge the deceased's 'diligent and active' virtues before unreservedly dedicating the remainder of his character portrait to Stoddard's inoffensive passivity, as per the sermon's primary scriptural motif:

> His short and inoffensive (and yet diligent and active) life, is a loud and earnest Sermon upon my text. [. . .] If he that offendeth not in a word is a perfect man indeed, must not the DECEASED appear to us? How lovely and endearing was he in his domestic relations? How just, righteous and faithful, in his dealings and in his Trusts! How courteous and grateful to his friends? Ready to oblige, and easily obliged! How pure form the world, it's [sic] passions frauds and lusts! Who has there been among us . . . more sincere and without offence . . . more harmless and without rebuke? Doing all things without murmuring and disputings in the midst of a crooked and perverse nation . . . We are witnesses how modestly, meekly, justly, and unblameably he behaved himself among us . . . Whom did the Deceased ever speak evil of? Or when did he backbite with his tongue? Or do evil against his neighbour?[46]

Colman's extended list of rhetorical questions emphasize the deceased's passivity and inoffensiveness to the extent that his brief initial reference to Stoddard's 'diligent and active life' is negated by them. Indeed, here the possibility of 'damning with faint praise', or at least mildly rebuking with faint praise, is readily present, since Stoddard's seemingly utter passivity in life obliges Colman to defend the deceased's conduct in terms which border on the defensive in tone:

> It may be the more active lives of some others may be more praise-worthy; more worthy to be esteemed, admired and imitated by us, more fruitful to the glory of God and the benefit of men than this more silent and retir'd temper. It may be that there are some good men in the Town, as inoffensive, and yet more active in doing good than the Deceased : GOD increase their number! Who being equally harmless yet may be more filled with the fruits of righteousness.[47]

The equation of active virtues with God's greater glory is mooted here, thereby casting some shadow on the blameless but utterly passive qualities of the deceased merchant Stoddard. There are, however, also some notable caveats to consider here. Vitally, Colman qualifies that any 'good men in the Town' who are 'more active in doing good than the Deceased' must also be assessed by the criteria of maintaining passive inoffensiveness, as upheld by the deceased, as well as being 'equally harmless'. Colman's carefully graduated speculations suggest that more active lives may be more praise-worthy, though not merely by virtue of being active. Finally, the 'good men in the Town' – those more active than Stoddard – are just that – men in the Town, not necessarily other merchants. At the very least, Colman's conclusive opinion of the deceased's character and conduct appears to be compromised by a determined effort to foreground the passivity of his deceased mercantile subject when alive, notwithstanding the brief opening reference to Stoddard's active and diligent qualities.

Colman's disproportionately high estimation of passive Christian virtues in his subject, the deceased merchant David Stoddard, echoes certain tendencies of characterization also apparent in the funeral sermons by Waker and Rogers, despite its later date, its colonial provenance and its conditional acknowledgement of potentially 'fruitful' active Christian virtues in the population at large 'in the Town'. All three ministers present a lopsided portrait of the early modern merchant, overwhelmingly favouring the passive Christian virtues of their deceased subjects. This suggests the published funeral sermon presents a category of public commemoration in print unlike other contemporary portraits of merchants, whether idealized, fictional or autobiographical. This even seems to be the case whether ministers celebrate, or castigate, active and diligent conduct in other realms of endeavour (including naval warfare, spiritual integrity or the efforts of 'good men in the Town'). If this observation allows us to conclude little more than, ultimately, ministers decline to tell us the 'whole story' when commemorating deceased merchants in published funeral sermons, it simultaneously reveals new facets of the morally complex, profit-driven and publicly censured print culture in which such ministers participated.

Notes

1. On the early modern published funeral sermon, see Ralph Houlbrooke's chapter 'The Age of Decency: 1660–1760', in Peter C. Jupp and Clare Gittings (eds), *Death in England: An Illustrated History* (Manchester, 1999), pp. 187ff. See also Penny Pritchard's chapter 'The Protestant Funeral Sermon in England, 1688–1800', in Keith A. Francis and William Gibson (eds), *The Oxford Handbook of the British Sermon 1689–1901* (Oxford, 2012), pp. 322–37. Julien Litten reviews post-Reformation liturgical reforms to burial services in *The English Way of Death: The Common Funeral Since 1450* (London, 1991), pp. 151–8.
2. Calculation of precise numbers of published funeral sermons remains notoriously difficult, not least because of the widespread practice of anthologizing ministers' 'collected works', reprints under different titles, or reworking of texts to commemorate different deceased subjects. Though hardly definitive, approximate numbers may be derived from strategic searches on *Early English Books Online/Eighteenth-Century Collections Online* (forthwith EEBO/ECCO). Using the search-term 'funeral sermon' under category 'all' for the chronological period 1660–1800, the combined databases yield 6,628 titles, whereas 'funeral sermon' searched under the category 'title' yields only 1,101 titles for the same period. Using 'funeral' and 'sermon' to search under the respective categories of 'title' and 'genre' yields 205 titles for the same period.
3. Also cited in King James Version Mark 10:23–7 and Luke 18:25–7. Matthew Henry comments, 'with God all things are possible. This is a great truth in general, that God is able to do that which exceeds all created power; that nothing is too hard for God, Genesis 18:14; Numbers 11:23.' Matthew Henry, *An Exposition of the Historical Books of the New Testament* (London, 1725), vol. 5, pp. 137 ff.
4. Max Weber, *The Protestant Ethic and the Spirit of Capitalism*, trans. Stephen Kalberg (New York and Oxford, 2011). Two excellent sources which briefly summarize key aspects of the Weberian debate include the chapter entitled 'An Active Frame in Courts Below', in Matthew Kadane, *The Watchful Clothier: The Life of an Eighteenth-Century Protestant Capitalist* (New Haven and London, 2013), pp. 84–10; Patrick Collinson, 'Religion, Society, and the Historian', in *The Journal of Religious History*, 23:2 (June 1999), 149–68.
5. Weber, *The Protestant Ethic*, p. 158.
6. Weber, *The Protestant Ethic*, and Collinson, 'Religion, Society, and the Historian', 165ff.
7. Houlbrooke, 'The Age of Decency: 1660–1760', p. 188.
8. Direct reference to the deceased's material success in Protestant funeral sermons is,

predictably, limited and purposely couched in obscure language. On this point, see F. Tromly, '"According to sounde religion": the Elizabethan controversy over the funeral sermon', in *Journal of Medieval and Renaissance Studies*, 13 (1983), 293–312.

9. Perry Gauci, *Emporium of the World: The Merchants of London 1660–1800* (London and New York, 2007). See in particular his Preface and chs 1 and 2, pp. 1–36.
10. John McVeagh, *Tradefull Merchants: The Portrayal of the Capitalist in Literature* (London, 1981), p. 45.
11. Daniel Defoe, Letter V, in *The Complete English Tradesman in Familiar Letters* [. . .] (London, 1726), pp. 55–6.
12. Defoe's fictional works further demonstrate cases where godly merchants or tradesmen happily resolve these dilemmas; see, for example, the master of apprentice Tom in book three of *The Family Instructor* (1722); Moll's final state of grace at the conclusion of *Moll Flanders* (1722), and Roxana's London financier in *Roxana* (1726).
13. Anonymous, *Character and Qualification of an Honest Loyal Merchant* (London, 1686), p. 12.
14. Anonymous, *Character and Qualification of an Honest Loyal Merchant*, pp. 10–12.
15. Anonymous, *Character and Qualification of an Honest Loyal Merchant*, pp. 10–11. The work cited therein is William Peyt's anonymously attributed *Britannia Languens, or a Discourse of Trade* [. . .] (London, 1680).
16. Kadane, *The Watchful Clothier*, p. 1.
17. Kadane, *The Watchful Clothier*, pp. 1–3, 6–14. Here and throughout his text, Kadane offers a comprehensive discussion of past and recent scholarship on the early modern spiritual autobiography.
18. Kadane, *The Watchful Clothier*, ch. 1. See also Paul S. Seaver, *Wallington's World : A Puritan Artisan in Seventeenth-Century London* (Stanford, 1985), regarding the complex dual purpose of spiritual diaries (for private use and posterity), but see also Kadane, *The Watchful Clothier*, pp. 86–7, on the extent to which Joseph Ryder presents Weber's (necessarily externally realized) 'ideal-typical Protestant capitalist'.
19. John McVeagh, *Tradefull Merchants: The Portrayal of the Capitalist in Literature* (London, 1981), p. 36.
20. Daniel Defoe, Introduction to *The Family Instructor, Volume One*, facsimile reproduction ed. Paula Backscheider (Delmar, New York, 1989), pp. 2–3.
21. Carol Stewart, *The Eighteenth-Century Novel and the Secularization of Ethics* (Farnham, Surrey and Burlington, VT, 2010), p. 1.
22. Houlbrooke, 'The Age of Decency: 1660–1760', p. 188.
23. Anonymous, *A Letter from an Old Merchant to his Son* (Dublin, 1753), pp. 17–18.
24. Anonymous, *A Letter from an Old Merchant*, pp. 15–16.
25. Anonymous, *Character and Qualification of an Honest Loyal Merchant*, pp. 2–3.
26. Anonymous, *Character and Qualification of an Honest Loyal Merchant*, p. 3.
27. Gauci, *Emporium of the World*, p. 101.
28. Gauci, *Emporium of the World*, p. 101.
29. Further exploratory searches on EEBO/ECCO offer a broad indication of the extant print record. Using the term 'merchant' under the search category of 'title' and 'funeral' under either 'subject' or 'genre' returned 22 hits for all texts on the databases (covering, in total, the chronological period 1473–1800). While a search employing 'merchant' under the category 'title' and 'funeral' under the broader 'all' search category produced 128 hits, these texts include plays with the title 'Merchant' in them or sermons preached before the Merchant-Taylors School.

30 Thomas Brooks, *A String of Pearles: or, The best things reservd till last* [...] (London, 1657); Joseph Hill, *The Providence of God in sudden Death ordinary and extraordinary vindicated and improved* [...] (Rotterdam, 1685); Edmund Batson, *A funeral sermon on the death of Mrs. Mary Paice, late wife of Mr. Joseph Paice Merchant of Clapham* [...] (London, 1700); Charles Chauncy, *A Funeral Discourse on the Death of Mrs. Lucy Waldo, The amiable Consort of Mr. Samuel Waldo, Merchant in Boston* [...] (Boston, 1741). The prevalence of early modern published funeral sermons for the wives of eminent or high-profile individuals merits separate investigation; on the topic of typologies of subject in funeral sermons, see the chapter by Penny Pritchard, 'Speaking Well of the Dead': Characterisation in the Early Modern Funeral Sermon', in Liisa Steinby and Aino Mäkikalli (eds), *Speaking Well of the Dead: Narratological Concepts in the Study of Eighteenth-Century Literature* (Amsterdam, 2017).

31 Evelyn E. Cowie, 'Colwall, Daniel (d. 1690)', *Oxford Dictionary of National Biography*, (Oxford, 2004); online edn January 2008, http://www.oxforddnb.com/view/article/6014, accessed 3 May 2016; Perry Gauci, 'Thomas, Sir Dalby (c.1650–1711)', *Oxford Dictionary of National Biography* (Oxford, 2004); online edn January 2008, http://www.oxforddnb.com/view/article/49984, accessed 3 May 2016.

32 D. W. Jones, 'Herne, Sir Joseph (bap. 1639, d. 1699)', rev. Anita McConnell, *Oxford Dictionary of National Biography* (Oxford, 2004); online edn January 2008, http://www.oxforddnb.com/view/article/37537, accessed 3 May 2016.

33 Gauci, *Emporium of the World*, p. 97; David Hancock, *Citizens of the World* (Cambridge, 1995). On the subject of merchants' active involvement in charitable and religious activities, see also Natasha Glaisyer, 'Networking: Trade and Exchange in the Eighteenth-Century British Empire', in *The Historical Journal*, 47:2 (June 2004), 451–76.

34 Daniel Defoe, *A Hymn to the Funeral Sermon* (London, 1703), p. 2.

35 John Dunton, *The Hazard of a Death-Bed Repentance, Fairly Argued* (London, 1708), pp. i–ii.

36 This reflects the standard format for Protestant funeral sermons; on this subject see Tromly, '"According to sounde religion"', 306, 311; Clare Gittings, *Death, Burial and the Individual in Early Modern England* (London, 1984), pp. 137–8.

37 Nathanael Waker, *A Sermon Preached at the Funerall of Mr. Lucas Lucie, Merchant* [...] (London, 1664); Timothy Rogers, *The Changableness [sic] of this World. With Respect to Nations, Families, and particular Persons* (London, 1692); Benjamin Colman, *A Blameless and Inoffensive Life* [...] *Preached on the Lord's Day after the funeral of the Virtuous and Exemplary Mr. David Stoddard of Boston, Merchant* (Boston, 1723). Colman also quotes from the first and third Epistles of John on the title page of Stoddard's funeral sermon.

38 Waker, *A Sermon*, p. 4.

39 Waker, *A Sermon*, p. 34.

40 Waker, *A Sermon*, pp. 36–7.

41 Waker, *A Sermon*, p. 39.

42 Rogers, *The Changableness [sic] of this World*, Epistle Dedicatory.

43 Rogers, *The Changableness [sic] of this World*, pp. 97–9.

44 Rogers, *The Changableness [sic] of this World*, pp. 106–11.

45 Rogers, *The Changableness [sic] of this World*, Epistle Dedicatory.

46 Colman, *A Blameless and Inoffensive Life*, pp. 31–2.

47 Colman, *A Blameless and Inoffensive Life*, p. 33.

MARY'S MAGNIFICAT IN EIGHTEENTH-CENTURY BRITAIN AND NEW ENGLAND

Laura M. Stevens

It is unsurprising that the 1759 Battle of Quebec, in which the British and their allies scaled cliffs over the city of Quebec to vanquish the French and indigenous forces, tilting the Seven Years' War towards British victory, occasioned much rejoicing in Britain and its colonies. Amidst more decorous commemorations, ranging from thanksgiving sermons to Benjamin West's famous painting of the death of General Wolfe, are less restrained ones, such as *A Brief Review of the Campaigns in America, from the Year 1755 to 1760*. This collection of eight poems, published in Boston and authored by Joseph Fisk, crows over the vanquishing of the French, and it does so with gleeful recourse to several clichés of anti-Catholic ideology, in which Roman Catholicism is marked as a perversion of Protestantism's rightness and truth. In the lead-up to the battle, for example, Fisk reports, 'Our Foes rejoice and shout aloud, / And *Antichrist* grows very proud', and of the victory he declares, '*Popedom* . . . was brought in thral.'[1] Fisk does not content himself with attacking French troops but extends his rhetoric to the civilian population of Quebec, especially its women. Openly gloating over their fear and grief, he combines a traditional condemnation of female vanity with another stock element of anti-Catholicism, an attack on prayers to the Virgin Mary and beliefs that Mary can pray to God on behalf of the humans who seek her aid:

> Will they now paint or curl their Hair,
> When Death doth in their Faces stare ?—
> Or, will they to the *Virgin* cry,
> O Virgin ! *save us, or we die* !
> O Virgin-Mary, *can't you save*
> *Our Souls from sinking in the Grave;*
> Or, yet at least, to set us by,
> Or pray us out of Purgat'ry!*[2]

Both their primping and their pleas to Mary – prayers that to Protestants smacked of idolatry –link these bereaved and terrified women to another mainstay of anti-Catholic ideology, the inclination to read the Whore of Babylon from Revelation chapter 17 as a symbol of the Roman Catholic Church. Here, the link is a deliberate attack on women, rather than abstract. The Whore here does not just stand for the Roman Church, the pope, or behaviours redolent of so-called popery, as she so often did in anti-Catholic rhetoric.[3] Rather, she has daughters who, as Revelation 17:6 specifies of the Whore, drink the blood of the saints:

> Proud *Babel's* Daughters must be doom'd,
> And in dark Regions be entomb'd:
> The Blood of Saints they once did spill,
> And now of Blood they drink their fill.[4]

Simply because they are French and Catholic, qualities evidenced most audibly in their prayers to Mary, these women are to be condemned to 'entomb[ment]'. Such are the wages of the sins of errant belief, membership in an enemy nation, and flawed prayer.

If Fisk's poem was unusual in its viciousness, it was all too standard in its inclination to condemn Roman Catholics for praying to Mary. Six decades earlier, for example, Increase Mather, famous Puritan minister of Massachusetts Bay colony, had dismissed belief in Mary's power of intercession by reasoning, 'As for the *Papists*, there are Thousands, it may be Millions of them, praying at once to the *Virgin Mary*; its [*sic*] impossible that she being a Creature only should hear all those prayers at once.'[5] To pray to Mary, from Mather's perspective, was to deny her humanity, and to veer into a ludicrous level of gullibility. To do so also was to risk egregious sin. Two years earlier, Mather had gone so far as to assert that the Devil 'hath often appeared in the Form of the *Virgin Mary*, whereby miserable Souls have been seduced into gross Idolatries'.[6] Praying to Mary was so dangerous that it could make one more vulnerable to the Devil's trickery.

Nor were New England Puritans the only Protestants who condemned prayer to Mary. *The Principles of the Christian Religion Explained*, a catechism of 1752 authored by a 'Clergyman of the Church of Ireland', illustrates much of what was at stake in Protestant discussions of Mary:

> Q. What think you of those, who pay divine Worship to her, on Account of this miraculous Conception and Birth?
> A. I believe them to be guilty of the grossest Idolatry . . .
> Q. Is it not proper to pay some extraordinary Respect to the Mother of our Lord?
> A. It is; on this Account we should honour her Name, when Mention is made of it, endeavour to imitate her great Virtues, and account it an extraordinary Honour that God was pleased to confer on her, that she shou'd be the Mother of our Lord and Saviour Jesus Christ, according to the Flesh.[7]

With the Virgin Mary, there were boundaries not to be crossed. Above all, one must not pray *to* her, seeking her intercession with God. To take this step was to cross over from respect to worship, from honour to idolatry.

Praying *like* Mary, however, was a different matter. As Christine Peters has written, 'In the Reformation of the sixteenth and early seventeenth centuries, . . . attacks on the Virgin Mary led to a redefinition of her significance rather than to her disappearance.' Above all, the Protestant inclination was to diminish her role as God's mother and emphasize her position as Christ's first follower.[8] If this reclamation of Mary was stalled in late seventeenth-century England, when fears of a Catholic king amplified anti-Catholic rhetoric, it is also clear that in the wake of the Glorious Revolution, with the coronation of James II's solidly Protestant daughter and son-in-law and then Parliament's settlement of the throne on the Protestant house of Hanover, there was an abatement of anti-Catholicism from its highest levels. Even as the penal code against Catholics continued for well over a century, theological and devotional writings in Britain and its colonies evidenced a modulation of attitude towards Mary that suggests less an effort to banish her than to make her safe for Protestants. They did so largely through presenting Mary as a model of prayerful devotion, seen most of all in the one prayer the Bible attributes to her: the Magnificat.

* * *

The Magnificat, Mary's song of praise to God, is recorded in Luke 1:46–55. It is uttered by Mary after her cousin Elizabeth has greeted her in words later incorporated into the Ave Maria, or Hail Mary, a prayer central to Roman Catholic devotional practices such as the rosary: 'Blessed are you among woman, and blessed is the fruit of thy womb.'[9] The opening lines of Mary's response to Elizabeth are worth quoting in full:

> My soul doth magnify the Lord,
> And my spirit hath rejoiced in God my Saviour.
> For he hath regarded the low estate of his handmaiden: for, behold, from henceforth all generations shall call me blessed.
> For he that is mighty hath done to me great things; and holy is his name.[10]

This prayer, which has a close relationship to the songs of Deborah in Judges chapter five and Hannah in I Samuel chapter one, has been central to Protestant regard of Mary since the beginning of the Reformation. As Peters has noted, 'Luther's commentary on the Magnificat validated this text as suitable for protestants, but he was careful to distance it from Catholic emphases. He focused on Mary's lowliness and humility and advised people to 'not make too much of calling her "Queen of Heaven".'[11] Through such a reading Luther sought to make Mary an exemplum of piety rather than an object of intercession.

Luther's stamp of approval did not save the Magnificat from attack, especially in peak episodes of anti-Catholic panic. John Oldham's satires on the Jesuits, written in response to the Popish Plot of 1679–80, provide an especially colourful example. The third satire, claiming to be Ignatius of Loyola's will, contains these commands for the Jesuit order:

> Tell how the blest *Virgin* to come down was seen,
> Like *Play-House Punk* descending in *Machine*:
> How she writ *Billets Doux*, and *Love-Discourse*,
> Made *Assignations*, *Visits*, and *Amours*: . . .
> Relate . . .
> How *Pigs* to th' *Rosary* kneel'd, and *sheep* were taught
> To bleat *Te Deum* and *Magnificat*.[12]

These vivid lines intertwine a few well-established strands of anti-Catholic rhetoric: first, the linking of Catholicism with sexual promiscuity, perversion and whoredom; second, the equating of the cult of the Virgin with idolatry, intensified here by intimations of incest;

and third, the depiction of Catholicism as a false religion that peddles superstition to the ignorant, requiring so little exercise of reason that even animals can be trained in its rituals and rote prayers. The Marian origin of the Magnificat, as well as, no doubt, its neat fit into the iambic metre and close rhyme with 'taught', provides the punch, as it were, to this comic line.

Attacks on Roman Catholics through this prayer at times were extended to critiques of the Church of England by Nonconformists. The Baptist Thomas DeLaune's *Plea for the Non-Conformists*, first published in 1683 and then reprinted after his death in 1704, condemned the Book of Common Prayer for its 'Similitude . . . with the Form of Prayer which the Papists used'. DeLaune specifically protested against the use of set prayers in the liturgy including 'the Psalms, *Venite, Benedictus, Magnificat, nunc Dimittis*, . . . of which we can give no good Reason'. The scriptural origin of these prayers did not allay his sense that they had been 'abused unto Idolatry and Superstition by the Papists', and thus were in a sense contaminated beyond repair.[13] Similarly, *A Dialogue between a Curat [sic] and a Country-Man, Concerning the English-Service, or Common-Prayer-Book of England*, by John Anderson, a minister of the Church of Scotland, expressed fears that the Church of England's Book of Common Prayer would be imposed on the Presbyterian Church of Scotland. In this dialogue the Country-Man complains, 'There are some leading Terms in the Service Book, such as . . . *magnificat, nunc dimittis, Te Deum* . . . &c. I think they are neither ENGLISH nor PLAIN ENGLISH, nor do I believe every Body understands them.'[14] Later, the Country-Man disputes the Curate's assertion 'that the Primitive Christians prayed by a FORM'. Two concerns thus emerge from these complaints: first, that the Magnificat is not accessible to less educated believers, and second, that as a set or scripted prayer it is not in keeping with the devotional practices of the 'primitive' or early Church. *The Beauty of Holiness in the Common Prayer*, a short pamphlet published in 1752, voiced related if far more muted concerns about the Magnificat. This text's opinion that 'The *magnificat*, and *nunc dimittis*, seem very improper for Christian worship', seemed to fit within the author's assertion that 'our daily services . . . do very much want to be reviewed and amended'.[15] For those who sought a simpler, shorter, more accessible liturgy, whether more radical Dissenters or Conformists who nonetheless were strongly opposed to a High Church stance, this prayer could be objectionable.

The Magnificat, along with other references to Mary, additionally hazarded some association with more radical eighteenth-century groups such the Philadelphian Society, which anchored prophecies and devotional practices to women's corporeality that were alarming to more mainstream Protestants. Richard Roach's *The Crisis*, which articulated his millennialist prophecies, argued for example of John the Baptist, 'His Mother was a *Prophetess* also; shown in her Inspir'd Re-Salutation, and Predictive Blessing to the *Virgin Mary*; to which *She* also Responded in her *Magnificat*.'[16] For Roach, the Magnificat was not just a song of praise to God, but also a prophecy, as was the greeting of her cousin Elizabeth.

Still, across the early modern period most anglophone Protestant responses to the Magnificat show no significant break from the basic elements of Luther's commentary. It is noteworthy that John Foxe's *Acts and Monuments*, colloquially known as the *Book of Martyrs*, describes one of the Marian martyrs, Roger Clark, kneeling in 1546 to recite this prayer immediately after he 'with most strong and vehement words, rebuked that idolatrye and supersticion', when he was asked to kneel before a passing procession.[17] Clark's message was that a Christian should kneel only before God; far from suggesting popery, Mary's prayer conveyed for this Protestant martyr the reverence that a true believer should demonstrate only for God.

The prominence of English translations of important Lutheran theological and devotional writings, such as a 1716 publication in London of Johann Arndt's *The Garden of Paradise; or, holy prayers and exercises, whereby the Christian graces and virtues may be planted and improved in man* (1716), reinforces that continuity. In this text Arndt cited the Magnificat as an example of the degree of prayer in which 'a Man prays with great Joy and Exultation of Heart'.[18] Above all, this song of praise, which constitutes a central element of the Evening Prayer in the Church of England's Book of Common Prayer, proves central to an understanding of Mary less as the physical vessel of God than as Christ's first witness and most exemplary believer, noteworthy above all for her acceptance of God accompanied by her abnegation of self. An increasingly disembodied Mary came to stand as synecdoche for Christian belief, providing a point of commonality between Conformists to and Dissenters from the Established Church. In this way Mary's song of praise proved central to a key dialectic of Enlightenment, articulating the importance of belief itself, especially an internally directed form of belief, in response to what many believers perceived as the rising threats of deism, atheism, or merely diminished faith.

A wide range of writings from the eighteenth century similarly used the Magnificat to emphasise an Enlightenment form of piety simultaneously anchored in joyous faith, scriptural knowledge, and reason. John Clutterbuck's *Plain and Rational Vindication and Explanation of the Liturgy of the Church of England*, a catechism first published in the seventeenth century, rather candidly justified the inclusion of hymns such as the Magnificat in the liturgy on the grounds that 'by this variety People are secured against Weariness and Distraction', even as they 'benefit . . . from the Word of God'. The Magnificat in particular teaches its listeners 'Examples of God's Mercy, and . . . Prophecies and Promises which are now fulfill'd in Christ's Birth'. Perhaps its greatest purpose, though, is to prompt its listeners and singers to praise God just as Mary did, so that 'we may be expected to rejoice with her in the same Words'.[19] Christians thus are directed to think of themselves as imitating Mary in their prayer while they also join with her in praising God. Charles Wheatly's *The Church of England Man's Companion* (1710), known for its High Church approach to the liturgy, shared much with Clutterbuck's interpretation. Emphasizing the prayer's age and universality through his insistence that the Magificat 'hath . . . been anciently us'd among Christians, and is still retain'd amongst all the *Reform'd* Churches beyond Sea as well as ours', he explained its expected effect on listeners: 'so we, when we hear in the Lessons like Examples of his Mercy, and are told of those Prophecies and Promises which are now fulfill'd in Christ's Birth, may very properly rejoice with her in the same words'.[20] The purpose of the Magnificat was to serve as a model and inspiration for believers as they expressed their awareness of, and gratitude for, God's blessings.

This understanding of the Magnificat as a prompt to imitative prayer is sometimes visible even when the prayer is not named. For example, as part of its 'Short, Devotional Exercises' for the Festival of the Annunciation, *The Christian's Memorandum-Book; or, Family Instructor*, which advertised itself as based on the Church of England's liturgy, offered the following prayer:

> We beseech thee, O Lord, pour thy Grace into our Hearts, that as we have known the Incarnation of thy Son Jesus Christ, by the Message of an Angel; so by his Cross and Passion, we may be brought unto the Glory of his Resurrection.[21]

Although not referencing the Magnificat directly, this collect, with its petition that 'Grace' be 'pour[ed] ... into our Hearts', evokes a central conceit of Mary's prayer: an awareness of the transcendent and intangible divinity made present in the individual believer. Interestingly, a Roman Catholic catechism first published in 1649 but reprinted in the eighteenth century, Henry Turberville's *An Abridgment of Christian Doctrine*, took pains to note that the reverence typically expressed when the Magnificat was sung in the liturgy was directed at the Scripture and not Mary:

> Q. *Why do we stand up at the* Magnificat, Benedictus, *and* Nunc dimittis?
> A. To signify our Reverence to the Gospel, whence they are taken.

Lest there be any confusion, Turberville made clear in the next answer, about collects, that prayers are to Jesus Christ as 'our only Mediator of Redemption', while '*The Virgin* Mary *prays in the Name of her Son*'.[22] Through such comments Turberville, in what came to be known as the Douay catechism, after the place of its initial publication, sought to rebut a standard Protestant criticism of Roman Catholic devotional practice.[23]

* * *

Although there is continuity in the basic interpretation of the Magnificat and its devotional function, shifts in the anglophone rephrasing of the song provide a useful index to gauging alterations in how Christian belief is understood and articulated over the course of the century. The Nonconformist theologian and hymn writer Isaac Watts stands at the opening of what developed into a relatively widespread tradition of poetic scriptural paraphrase in Britain, breaking away from fairly strict reiterations of scriptural verses and adherence to ballad metre. His version of the Magnificat in *Hymns and Spiritual Songs*, first published in 1707, adheres to the basic elements of Luther's response to Mary. Song 60, 'The Virgin Mary's Song; or the Promised Messiah Born', positions a Christian congregation, designated by the first-person plural, in the act of self-consciously and deliberately imitating Mary's prayer:

> Our Souls shall magnifie the Lord,
> In God the Saviour we rejoice:
> While we repeat the Virgin's Song,
> May the same Spirit tune our Voice.

Even as the singers 'repeat' after Mary, seeking to praise God in the words and even tune she used, Watts is scrupulous in distinguishing between admiration and adoration, an approach that of course was regarded as idolatrous and Roman Catholic. As his third stanza asserts:

> Let every Nation call her Blest,
> And endless Years prolong her Fame
> But God alone must be adored,
> Holy and Reverend is his Name.

Echoing Elizabeth's words to her cousin, 'blessed art thou', the congregation proclaims its own insistence on drawing the theological line between Mary and God, marking the latter as an object of belief and worship, while the former stands as a model of belief.

John Wesley's *Hymns and Sacred Poems*, first published in 1739, displays continuity with the approach of Watts even as it also presents a clear departure in affect and in the construction of personal piety. While Watts's hymn called the congregation to regard and repeat Mary's song, Wesley's provides no mediation between the congregation and Mary. His hymn immediately and directly imitates Mary's voice, beginning:

> My Soul extols the mighty Lord,
>   In God the Saviour joys my Heart:
> Thou hast not my low State abhor'd;
>   Now know I, Thou my Saviour art.[24]

The stylistic differences between Wesley and Watts are immediately clear. Through the Magnificat Wesley articulates a highly personal, individualistic and emotional form of belief. Rather than collectively regarding Mary, proclaiming as a group that they are imitating her song even as they assure themselves that they are not adoring or praying to her, the singers of Wesley's version place themselves exactly in Mary's position, singing what she sings, magnifying God in their souls just as she does. Instead of ranging into theological commentary, this version of the song engages in emotional elaboration, with a richly detailed affective response to God:

> Sorrows and Sighs are fled away,
>   Peace now I feel, and Joy and Rest:

> Renew'd I hail the Festal Day.
> Henceforth by endless Ages blest.[25]

The basic elements of Luke's verses surely are here, but they are presented in more modern language: 'sorrows and sighs are fled'. Such phrasing could be lifted out of a ballad or sentimental novel from this era. The wording of this hymn affirms Phyllis Mack's understanding of early Methodism as an outgrowth of the 'Pietist concept of "heart religion," which stressed passivity and feeling rather than reason and good deeds', along with an Enlightenment emphasis on measurable subjective experience. Within Methodism, Mack writes, 'The goal of the individual's religious discipline was to shape her personal desires and narrow self-interest until they became identical with God's desire, with absolute goodness.'[26] With its description of an individual soul brought to a state of 'Peace' and 'Joy' through rapturous praise of God, the Magnificat might qualify as a quintessentially Methodist expression of devotion. That the individual believer's perspective would be aligned with Mary's makes perfect sense, for it models the affective spirituality of Methodism, even as it fits a more general Protestant inclination to de-emphasize the Virgin's maternal body in contrast to her soul.

Later in the century Mary's prayer saw new versifications outside of hymn collections, and with this migration across genres came more dramatic alterations to the song's scripturally based phrasing. Thomas Drummond's *Poems Sacred to Religion and Virtue*, published in 1756, belied the author's prefatory claim to be offering 'a Mite into the Treasury of Religion and Virtue' by drawing upon the language of romance.[27] The first stanza of this Magnificat contains more passion than pious devotion, suggesting seduction by an earthly lover:

> My Soul, O Lord! with Rapture fill'd,
> Declares the Greatness of thy Name;
> My Heart exulting beats with Joy,
> And every Thought is rapt to Flame.[28]

If Drummond aimed for rapture, other poetic paraphrases of Mary's song sought to draw out more muted or explicitly pious feelings. James Elphinson, for example, included a version of the Magnificat in *A Collection of Poems,* which he billed as 'Peculiarly Designed to Form the Taste of Youth'. This version replaced the more traditional ballad stanza with couplets, and rather than speaking from Mary's perspective in first person it spoke to her as the recipient of God's blessing:

> Soul and spirit, heart and voice,
> Bless th' Almighty and rejoice
> In thy God, who from above
> View'd thee with auspicious love;
> And, descending to thy aid,
> Snatcht thee from oblivion's shade![29]

The simplicity of the vocabulary and phrasing in these couplets does seem to fit Elphinson's stated intention of targeting a young audience. The syncopation and rhyme scheme of this poem made it easy to memorize through straightforward repetition, while the relation it maps out between human and divine is both simpler and more subdued than that sketched by Drummond. Rather than singing in imitation of Mary, those who voice this poem effectively exhort Mary to rejoice and bless God as she is 'snatcht' into the spotlight of fame. Different as these two poems are in tone and form, however, they jointly evidence some drifting away from strict adherence to Scripture in favour of innovative rewordings. If Wesley's hymn indicated the rise of affective spirituality within British Christianity, these later poems suggest a subordination of scripturally inspired prayer to spiritually inflected affect and verbal craft. Religion increasingly is an inspiration and source for art, emotion and craft, rather than the other way around. In these non-liturgical renditions, Mary's song provides a vehicle for articulating feelings ranging from wonder to gratitude, experiences ranging from the quaint to the sublime.

* * *

The trajectory of the Magnificat was not entirely from the arena of collective worship and theological entrenchment to more personal forms of piety or aesthetic expression, however. A quick look at sermons and theological tracts from this century reinforces what the hymns and poems already suggest, which is some significant variation in the stylistics of piety attributed to Mary's song. At the same time, there is consistency in the elevation of the Magnificat as a prayer articulating the importance of belief within Protestantism, and of Mary as model believer. *The History of the Incarnation, Life, Doctrine, and Miracles* (1737), authored by a

'Divine of the Church of England', took the Magnificat to be evidence of Mary's reception of God's grace, but the grace that she passively exhibits is intertwined with her own comportment and faith:

> In this Ode the Blessed Virgin discovers such a Sense of the divine Honours with which she was favour'd, and at the same Time so fully testifies her Humility and Devotion, that it appears she was indeed full of Grace, and had a Soul plentifully enriched with the Gifts of God's holy Spirit.[30]

The complexity of this sentence's syntax creates a circle of mutual causality, so that Mary's 'Humility and Devotion' both follow from and evidence her being filled with grace.

The English clergyman Ferdinando Warner's *A Rational Defence of the English Reformation and Protestant Religion* offers a synthesis of Anglican attitudes to Mary at mid-century. Protestants are entirely unlike Catholics in their treatment of Mary, he asserts: 'If we look into [Catholic] churches, and view their pictures and images, there we every where see holy Mary with our saviour still an infant in her arms, as if he were always to be a child.' It was through discussion of the Magnificat that Warner pivoted specifically away from Catholic devotion, for 'We chuse rather to follow her example, and say, my soul doth magnify the lord.'[31] Connected to Whig patronage networks, Warner generally articulated a Low Church theology, and indeed this publication was largely an annotated compendium of extracts from the writings of 'moderate whigs who were installed in the 1690s, such as Tillotson and Stillingfleet'.[32] The biblical scholar Robert Holmes's tract 'On the Angelical Message to the Virgin Mary', from later in the century, also used Mary's prayer to advocate for a Christian faith grounded in reason: 'the hymn of praise, which Mary forthwith uttered, was not more rapturous in point of devotion, than it was reasonable in point of faith'.[33] For Holmes, Mary's prayer supported his understanding of Christianity as a religion removed from superstition, fanaticism, and ignorance.

This position seems to have cut across most Protestant confessions in Britain and British North America; indeed, a remarkably wide range of genres and writers from about 1690 seized on Mary as a model of faith and prayer. A funeral sermon of 1697 by the Presbyterian minister Timothy Rogers, for example, went so far as to cite favourably what 'a devout *Popish* Writer says of the *Blessed Virgin*, on her Reading attended

Meditation; on her Meditation Prayer; on her Prayer Action'.[34] Some Congregationalists in New England apparently were in agreement with the Presbyterians of London on this matter. Nathaniel Appleton, a minister in Cambridge, quoted Luke 1:46 on the title page of his funeral sermon for Martha Gerrish, a prominent matron of the area.[35] Benjamin Colman – known to be an admirer of John Tillotson's writings, which were widely regarded as exemplifying a Low Church, Latitudinarian form of Anglicanism – indicated as much when he wrote, in a collection of Sacramental Discourses:

> We must delight in Christ and *praise* him with joyful lips. When ... *Elizabeth* had met [Mary] with those words, *Whence is it that the mother of my Lord should come unto me? Mary* burst out, as well she might, *My soul doth magnify the Lord*.[36]

Such approaches made no quarrel with the treatment of the Magnificat in the *Book of Common Prayer*, even as the precise tenor of piety and faith they articulated through this song shows some variation. Even the Quaker Robert Barclay cited Martin Luther's words on the Magnificat, 'No man can rightly know God, or understand the word of God, unless he immediately receive it from the Holy Spirit', to support the Society of Friends' insistence on immediate Revelation.[37] That Luther would not have agreed with such a reading of his words does not diminish the very wide appeal that this prayer held for so many types of Protestants.

* * *

In an era of intense theological disagreement and grudging toleration, it seems that the exemplarity of the Magnificat, especially with its impeccable scriptural provenance, amounted to a rare subject upon which most Protestants could agree. Anglicans and Presbyterians alike could find nothing objectionable in the assertion of a Puritan such as Cotton Mather when he said, in a funeral sermon of 1697, 'You'll easily bring a *Christian*, to join in a Consort with the Song of *Mary*.'[38] The irreproachability of this prayer is suggested in less theologically precise terms by *The Club. In a Dialogue between Father and Son*, a humorous tract that ridicules stock 'Characters' who are 'merely intended to expose Vice, and Folly'. The character of the Critic appears in this dialogue as one who is 'wise enough (in his own Conceit) to correct the *Magnificat*;

pretending to exquisite Niceness, censur'd *Cicero* for being too Verbose, and *Virgil* for using Rustic Language'. The grouping of this prayer with the writings of Cicero and Virgil conveys the Magnificat's status in eighteenth-century Britain as a literary classic, if not a religious one. To seek to correct such a poem is to qualify oneself as an 'unmerciful Fault-finder: two steps above a Fool'.[39]

The increasingly prominent and only sporadically contested place of this text in the religious discourse of Britain and its colonies reminds us that amidst much religious discord, the Magnificat proved important as a raw assertion of the importance of belief articulated through prayer. In this sense Mary, so often seized upon in the seventeenth century as a symbol of all that Protestants despised in Roman Catholicism, emerged in the eighteenth as a banner spokeswoman of key elements of Protestant theology, most of all the unsurpassed importance of faith. As the mathematician and theologian Isaac Barrow said of Mary, in a sermon published decades after his death by John Tillotson:

> worthily she did in that respect acknowledge, that *God had done . . . magnificent and mighty things for her*; yet really, in just esteem, to have Christ born in her soul, to have participated of his divine grace and presence in her heart, was a nobler honour, and a truer happiness in that.[40]

Such a notion was hardly new, for Augustine had written of Mary, 'She kept the truth in God's mind, a nobler thing than carrying his body in her womb'.[41] Late seventeenth- and eighteenth-century English Protestants made the old new, however, in their focus on the Magnificat as a model for faith. Mary's status as Christ's mother was not unimportant, but she was to be revered for her exemplary belief. This belief was evident above all in her most famous prayer.

Obvious though such a point may sound, its importance should not be overlooked, especially at a time when Christians felt their faith to be newly assaulted by non-believers and when Protestant confessions underwent yet more fragmentation with the Great Awakening and Methodist Revival. To survey the Magnificat's treatment in the anglophone eighteenth century is thus to encounter several of the major components of the Enlightenment's engagement with religion, and of interactions among Protestants of different confessions and affective inclinations during this era. One key point of continuity emerges: during the Enlightenment a diverse array of British authors effectively made Mary safe for and crucial to Protestants, transforming her from Catholic icon into Christian voice. Perhaps the index subentry for 'Magnificat' in *Some Important Points of Primitive Christianity Maintained and Defended*, authored by George Bull, Bishop of St Davids, appropriately summarizes the eighteenth-century anglophone Protestant response to this Marian prayer: '*The Use of it not to be disliked*'.[42]

Notes

1. J. Fisk, *A Brief Review of the Campaigns in America, from the Year 1755 to 1760; With Other Remarkable Occurences which have Happen'd in Divine Providence, within the Space of that Time* (Boston, 1760), pp. 4, 28.
2. Fisk, *Brief Review*, p. 27. Italics in original.
3. L. M. Stevens, 'Healing a Whorish Heart: The Whore of Babylon and Protestant Interiority in Restoration and Eighteenth-Century Britain', in Y. M. Werner and J. Harvard (eds), *European Anti-Catholicism in a Comparative and Transnational Perspective. European Studies No. 31* (Amsterdam, 2013), pp. 71–84.
4. Fisk, *Brief Review*, p. 27. Italics in original.
5. I. Mather, *The Mystery of Christ Opened and Applyed* (Boston, 1686), p. 143.
6. I. Mather, *An Essay for the Recording of Illustrious Providences* (Boston, 1686), p. 218. To be fair, Mather also said the Devil could appear in the form of Christ, but without the attendant hazards of idolatry.
7. [By a Clergyman of the Church of Ireland], *The Principles of the Christian Religion Explained: in a Clear and Easy Comment on the Several Questions of our Church Catechism* (Dublin, 1752), pp. 36–7.
8. C. Peters, *Patterns of Piety: Women, Gender and Religion in Late Medieval and Reformation England* (Cambridge, 2003), p. 243.
9. King James Version, Luke 1:42.
10. King James Version, Luke 1:46–55.
11. Peters, *Patterns*, pp. 223–34.
12. J. Oldham, 'The Third Satyr upon the Jesuits. Loyola's Will', in *The Works of Mr. John Oldham, Together with his Remains* (7th edn, London, 1710), p. 35.
13. T. DeLaune, *De Laune's Plea for the Non-Conformists: Shewing the True State of their Case, and how Far the Conformists [sic] Separation from the Church of Rome for the Popish Superstitions, &c., Introduced into the Service of God, Justifies the Non-Conformist's Separation from them for the Same* (London, 1704), p. 35. On DeLaune's life and Baptist beliefs see M. A. G. Hayken, 'Thomas DeLaune', *Oxford Dictionary of National Biography* (Oxford, 2004).
14. J. Anderson, *A Dialogue between a Curat and a Country-Man, Concerning the English-Service, or Common-Prayer-Book of England* (Edinburgh, 1728), pp. 47, 54. The English Short-Title Catalogue records printings in 1711, 1728 and approximately 1750, as well as two sequel dialogues.

15. *The Beauty of Holiness in the Common Prayer, Set in a New and Just Light, and Many Objections to that Book, (After an Impartial Review) are Obviated and Removed. Humbly Attempted, for the Honour and Service of the Church of England, and the True Protestant Religion. By a Member of that Church* (London 1752), p. 13, Preface.
16. Richard Roach, *The Great Crisis: Or, the Mystery of the Times and Seasons Unfolded* (London, 1725), 159. Eighteenth-Century Collections Online. On the Philadelphian Society see Lionel Laborie, *Enlightening Enthusiasm: Prophecy and Religious Experience in Early Eighteenth-Century England* (Manchester, 2015).
17. J. Foxe, *Actes and Monuments of these Latter and Perilous Dayes* (London, 1563), bk 3, p. 711. This account was included in eighteenth-century reprintings and condensations such as H. Bilton, *The History of the English Martyrs* (London, 1720), p. 65.
18. J. Arndt, *The Garden of Paradise; or, holy prayers and exercises, whereby the Christian graces and virtues may be planted and improved in man* (London, 1716), p. xvi.
19. J. Clutterbuck, *A Plain and Rational Vindication and Explanation of the Liturgy of the Church of England, Collected out of the Discourses of some of the Reverend Bishops and Doctors of the Same Church, by Way of Question and Answer* (3rd edn, Dublin, 1701), pp. 15–16. The English Short Title Catalogue lists the first edition in 1694.
20. C. Wheatly, *The Church of England Man's Companion; or a Rational Illustration of the Harmony, Excellence, and Usefulness of the Book of Common Prayer* (Oxford, 1710), 46. Richard Sharp notes that this text was 'markedly high church in emphasis', in 'Wheatly, Charles', *Oxford Dictionary of National Biography* (Oxford, 2004). Wheatly's text was in part a collection of extracts from influential Anglican writings, such as Thomas Comber's *A Companion to the Temple and the Closet* (1672).
21. [Clergyman of London], *The Christian's Memorandum-Book; or, Family Instructor . . . To which is Added, an Introduction . . . The Whole Collected from the Liturgy of the Church of England, and the Excellent Divines of the Church of England* (London, 1755), p. 134.
22. H. Turberville, *An Abridgment of Christian Doctrine; with Proofs of Scripture, for Points Controverted. Catechistically Explain'd, by way of Question and Answer* (London, 1717), p. 192.
23. On the Douay Catechism see T. Cooper, 'Henry Turberville', rev. D. Milburn, *Oxford Dictionary of National Biography* (Oxford, 2004).
24. J. Wesley, *Hymns and Sacred Poems* (3rd edn, London, 1739), p. 134.
25. Wesley, *Hymns*, p. 134.
26. P. Mack, *Heart Religion in the British Enlightenment: Gender and Emotion in Early Methodism* (Cambridge, 2008), pp. 13, 9–10.
27. T. Drummond, *Poems Sacred to Religion and Virtue* (London, 1756), p. xi.
28. Drummond, *Poems Sacred*, p. 140.
29. J. Elphinston, *A Collection of Poems, from the Best Authors: Adapted to Every Age, but Peculiarly Designed to Form the Taste of Youth* (London, 1764), p. 315.
30. *The History of the Incarnation, Life, Doctrine, and Miracles; the Death, Resurrection, and Ascension, of Our Blessed Lord and Saviour Jesus Christ* (London, 1737), p. 5.
31. F. Warner, *A Rational Defence of the English Reformation and Protestant Religion: in a Series of Discourses on the Most Essential Points of Controversy between Protestants and Papists. Compiled from the Works of the Most Eminent Divines of the Church of England* (London, 1752), p. 151.
32. N. Aston, 'Ferdinando Warner', *Oxford Dictionary of National Biography* (Oxford, 2004).
33. R. Holmes, *Four Tracts. I. On the Principle of Religion, as a Test of Divine Authority. II. On the Principle of Redemption. III. On the Angelical Message to the Virgin Mary. IV. On the Resurrection of the Body* (Oxford, 1788), p. 177.

34. T. Rogers, *The Character of a Good Woman, Both in a Single and Marry'd State, in a Funeral Discourse on Prov. 31.10. Who can find a vertuous Woman? for her Price is far above Rubies. Occasion'd by the Decease of Mrs. Elizabeth Dunton, Who Died May 28. 1697. With an Account of Her Life and Death; And Part of the Diary Writ with her own Hand* (London, 1697), preface.
35. N. Appleton, *A Discourse Occasioned by the Death of That Pious and Afflicted Gentlewoman Mrs. Martha Gerrish, Wife of Mr. Benjamin Gerrish, and Daughter of the Late Col. Foxcroft, Who Rested from all her Pains and Sorrows the 14th of April, 1736. Having newly completed the 48th Year of her Age*. Appended to *The Happiness of a Holy Life, Exemplified in the Sickness and Death of the Pious Mrs. Martha Gerrish* (London, 1740).
36. B. Coleman, *Some of the Glories of our Lord and Saviour Jesus Christ, Exhibited in Twenty Sacramental Discourses Preached at Boston in New England* (London, 1728), p. 14. Rick Kennedy notes, 'Colman was an avid reader of Archbishop Tillotson and the "latitudinarian" wing of Anglican thinkers who emphasised rationality and toleration among Protestants.' 'Benjamin Colman', *American National Biography Online*: www.anb.org/ (accessed 16 July 2017).
37. R. Barclay, *An Apology for the True Christian Divinity: Being an Explanation and Vindication of the Principles and Doctrines of the People Called Quakers* (8th edn, London, 1780), p. 23.
38. C. Mather, *A Good Man Making a Good End. The Life and Death, of the Reverend Mr. John Baily, Comprised and Expressed in a Sermon, on the Day of his Funeral. Thursday. 16.d. 10.m. 1697* (Boston, 1698).
39. J. Puckle, *The Club. In a Dialogue between Father and Son* (London, 1713), p. 11.
40. I. Barrow, *The Works of the Learned Isaac Barrow, . . . Published by Dr. John Tillotson. Vol. 2* (London, 1716), p. 266.
41. Augustine of Hippo, Sermo 25, 7–8: PL 46, 937–8.
42. G. Bull, *Some Important Points of Primitive Christianity Maintained and Defended; in Several Sermons and Discourses* (London, 1713). This collection was published after Bull's death in 1710, with a biography by Robert Nelson.

THE ORDER AND METHODS OF NOSEGAYS: MENTAL PRAYER IN FRANÇOIS DE SALES'S *INTRODUCTION À LA VIE DÉVOTE* (1609) AND ITS EIGHTEENTH-CENTURY ENGLISH ADAPTATIONS

Sabine Volk-Birke

I. Introduction

One of the most successful devotional manuals of the seventeenth and eighteenth centuries, the Bishop of Geneva's *Introduction à la vie dévote*, was specifically designed for the lay person with numerous secular employments. Its training programme for a mental life dominated by prayer and a social life based on charitable conduct was supposed to be fitted into an otherwise busy schedule, so as to transform the reader's whole mind and daily routines. Shortly after its publication in French, it was translated into English at Douai for a recusant audience. This is the beginning of a complex history of Catholic and Protestant English translations, adaptations, re-translations and editions in France and in Britain. Clearly, features like de Sales's Catholic sacramental bias or his references to the rosary would not find their way into Protestant adaptations, but the tailoring to Anglican audiences goes well beyond such elisions. On the other hand, the new 1762 translation from de Sales's final French edition[1] by Bishop Richard Challoner gives English readers access to an uncensored Catholic text.

These crossings of linguistic, national and denominational borders have a long tradition.[2] They grant insights into divisive theological issues, the fashioning of national identities, and different approaches to individual piety. Although there are shared traditions of teaching devotion which influence piety in more than one denomination, my assumption is that each religious community has their own ideas of the mental make-up and habits conducive to, or even necessary for the correct worship,

https://doi.org/10.16922/jrhlc.3.2.7

and thus the fitting frame of mind for this worship. The respective front matter of the French source text and the English Protestant adaptations by the printer Nicolas Okes in 1616, the editor Henry Dodwell in 1673, and the editor William Nicholls in 1701 is analysed in a separate publication.[3] In this paper I want to address the ways in which the *Introduction to a Devout Life* seeks to instruct its readers in the perfection of prayer by helping them to regulate their minds, looking at the assumptions they make on the nature of the mind, and which methods they suggest for its training accordingly. Besides looking at the successive stages of the mental training recommended in the *Introduction*, I shall concentrate on one major divisive subject, namely mental prayer, to illustrate my main point. At the same time, my investigation aims to answer the question if there are relevant differences between denominations in this respect. The results of this inquiry should contribute to a better understanding of the cross-overs performed by devotional literature in Europe. Analysing the way in which these texts deal with their readers' intellectual and volitional capacities will contribute to a more detailed understanding of the workings of textual communities in the enlightenment, and to a more detailed understanding of what was considered common ground between Catholic and Protestant piety in the seventeenth and eighteenth centuries in Britain. It will also shed light on concepts of the mind and the self that are held by different authors of devotional manuals in the enlightenment. This paper is part of a larger project on the literary and cultural impact of Christian prayer in the seventeenth and eighteenth centuries in Britain.

II. The Catholic source text

François de Sales's *Introduction à la vie dévote* emphasizes both prayer and virtue, but above all love, in his manual. He addresses his readers in a kind and encouraging tone, avoiding sentimentality as well as condescension. His accessible style with its homely metaphors and his renunciation of conspicuous intellectual or theological finesse speaks for his desire to resonate with the many – so much so that Henry Dodwell, mistaking elegant simplicity for intellectual poverty, calls the book 'principally calculated for the weaker sort', providing not information for the understanding, but only 'edification of [the] Affections'.[4]

The work is clearly structured, even though de Sales reorganized his material in the course of the first three editions. The first edition consists of three main parts: The first contains 'les avis et exercises requis' for guiding the soul from its first desire to lead a devout life to its 'entière résolution de l'embrasser'.[5] In one sense, this part *is* the *Introduction*: it leads the reader through a series of purgations and meditations to a full confession and firm resolution which is the beginning of a devout life. The second part addresses the issue from a different point of view: it wants to teach a way to make contact with God through prayer and the sacraments, above all the Eucharist. This part is already cross-referenced in the first part: if you do not know how to pray, or how to meditate, read part two. It also refers back to part one, which contains meditations and prayers that are now integrated into a mental training schedule. Part three addresses two more spiritual skills, essential for the path outlined in part one: here the devotee learns how to avoid sin and cultivate virtue.[6] The introduction can be read unilaterally, i.e. consecutively, as a devotional manual, but it can also be used multilaterally, like a reference work, where you find answers to individual problems that slow down or frustrate your mental and spiritual training programme.

Not surprisingly, the *Introduction* is steeped in Catholic devotional traditions and practice. First and foremost, the veneration of the Virgin Mary and the prayer cycle of the rosary stand out, as do references to the sacraments of confession and communion, including the doctrine of the real presence. Further, particular postures for prayer are discussed, as is the recommended reading of other devotional works by Catholic theologians, Church Fathers and saints. Many of these passages do not make it into the Protestant adaptations, particularly not into Nicholls's version, because they would be considered heretical, blasphemous or superstitious.

III. The Anglican adaptations

The Anglican versions, one published in 1673 in Dublin, made by Henry Dodwell, distinguished lay humanist scholar, theologian and Nonjuror, and one published in 1701, adapted by the clergyman William Nicholls, author of the well-read *Commentary on the Book of Common Prayer* (first edn 1701), relied on two different English translations. Dodwell took the expurgated Yakesley translation of 1616 published by Nicholas Okes as his point of departure; Nicholls made word-perfect use of the anonymous Paris translation (Tournai College, 1648), but omitted sometimes considerable parts of his source text. Both editors were prolific writers who took an active part in the theological and administrative debates of their day, so both would take the theological and doctrinal implications of de Sales's work (and its respective translations) very seriously. Both adaptations reveal differences in their conception of the devotee's practice and mind when compared to de Sales, but they also differ from each other.

The most immediately visible instance of this difference is the framing of the text. Henry Dodwell replaces de Sales's emotional *Dedicatory Prayer*, with its threefold exclamation of 'vive Jésus', imploring Jesus to live in his heart, as well as de Sales's fifteen-page *Preface*, with his own *Preface*, which runs to seventy-six pages. It constitutes not just a defence of the valuable aspects of de Sales's *Introduction*, but gives the reader learned comments on denominational differences and on reasons for toleration, spiced with references to authorities, providing a significant contrast to the plain style of the manual it introduces. William Nicholls is more anti-Catholic than Dodwell. He also omits the dedicatory prayer of the source text, and juxtaposes his treatise called 'The Rise and Progress of the Spiritual Books in the Romish Church' with de Sales's preface.[7] In this treatise Nicholls admits almost grudgingly that 'notwithstanding the great and deserved aversion which this Nation has to Popery, yet the Books of Their Divines upon Devotional and Practical Subjects, have met with as favourable reception among Us, as if the Authors had been of a better Religion' (p. 3). The quality of these books worries Nicholls, because they tempt Protestants to 'have a pretty good Opinion of a very bad Religion' (p. 4). He fears the affection which these books evoke in readers' hearts, because an increase of affection, he argues, weakens judgement, so that many faults in these books can be overlooked.

Both Anglican authors deal with their source text differently. In general, Nicholls cuts out greater chunks than Dodwell and is less prepared to make small changes in order to tone down controversial passages. In principle, both agree on retaining substantial parts of their source's training programme. The mental progression to really devout prayer can be achieved when the devotee follows a set sequence of preparation, considerations, affections, and resolutions. Readers are challenged to use their memory, their understanding, and their will – the traditional array of faculties of the soul – in these steps. But they are also encouraged to use their imagination, particularly in an element of the preparation that is known as creation of place: a vivid mental scene, usually taken from an event in the life of Christ. Considerations are based on the understanding, as all three, de Sales, Dodwell and Nicholls, emphasize.[8] What is meant by considerations can be seen in the first part of the *Introduction*, where each meditation comes with considerations, affections and resolutions. They cover many aspects of human existence on earth, in relation to God, and relate to issues treated in a catechism, such as the purpose of human existence, or an appreciation of God's infinite goodness, or the gift of life to the individual believer. In this context, de Sales advises his readers to feel free in choosing the subject matter on which they want to meditate, as they need to explore the options they have and find the one which yields most spiritual fruit. Although the rational part of the mind must make these choices, the effect of the considerations is not purely intellectual. The process of finding fruitful considerations is designed to yield taste, fruit and light, and is compared to a bee gathering honey. So although the explicit reference is to the understanding, the mental process is still related to pleasurable sensual experience.[9]

These considerations are designed to move the affections towards God and matters of the faith. The term 'affections' does not mean tenderness or liking; it refers rather, more generally, to a mental tendency or disposition, an inclination towards something, which can be good or bad. The will, and practice, are called for here, as the virtuous affections need to be nurtured, while the sinful ones need to be curbed. De Sales explicitly distinguishes the purpose of rousing the affections from a desire to acquire knowledge or to discuss theology. Training the affections requires a conscious effort that involves the intellect and the emotions; its aim is first understanding the faith and then living it in love and charity.

The considerations should lead to the next step, which involves the will again: a resolution very practically related to one's daily life. It must be chosen to correct a particular shortcoming, weakness or sin, so there is a direct relation to the individual devotee's capacity to improve her mind and her actions. Finally, in the conclusion, the believer must thank God for all his blessings and offer him their affections and resolutions, so that they can then ask for his help in carrying out their good intentions. De Sales includes the option that they can pray for other people, too. Only at the end of all these mental exercises does he advise set prayers, namely an Our Father and a Hail Mary.

In the following chapter, however, de Sales seems to take back almost everything he has explained about the logical sequences of mental exercises for training proper devotion. He assumes that the practice of his readers may be different from this theory, as the individual steps that were so carefully outlined may not correspond to the believer's reality. Prayer can happen very differently: it is possible that the affections arise much earlier and do not wait for the considerations to be completed. In such cases, if his reader finds herself 'toute émue en Dieu' immediately after the preparation, de Sales allows his pupil the freedom to accept the pace her mind and emotion set for her. He compares this situation to a rider whose horse runs faster than intended: the rider is to let the reins loose. He explains that he took these several steps apart academically, as it were, in order to explain them clearly and intelligibly, but that they do not need to be followed in this very sequence if the mind arrives at the relevant point faster.[10] However, the resolutions are necessary every time. They need to come after the affections, as they are the goal and purpose of every prayer. So there is some order in these meditations and prayers that needs to be observed, but there is also room for individual situations and reactions, in which readers need to rely on their own judgment.

IV. A divisive issue: mental prayer in Catholic and Protestant devotion

So far, I have outlined the approach largely common to the Catholic and the Protestant versions of the text. One central issue where they each part company in different ways is the practice of mental prayer, a major point of dissent among denominations.[11] Dodwell explicitly approves of mental prayer[12] and retains virtually all passages that refer to it. Nicholls, on the other hand, criticises de Sales's teaching of mental prayer severely and denounces it as enthusiasm. For him, 'Mental Prayer and placing ones self in the Presence of God, which in the Mystical Cant signifies to divest our Mind of all kind of thought and desire, and to leave the Holy Ghost to inspire into the Mind what he thinks fit' is unacceptable.[13] In his brief historical review of devotional books he chastises particularly St Teresa of Avila's four steps on the way to mystical union with God, rounding up his account with 'This is enough for a Tast [sic] of the Bedlam Divinity'.[14] The contrast of theological opinion on this point marks Dodwell and Nicholls also as having different anthropological and philosophical concepts of human nature.

Since mental prayer is the cause of so much antagonism, we need to ask what it is and what it does to the human mind. In contrast to vocal prayer, which relies on set forms and communal words, mental prayer is not only silent and individual, it can even be wordless. It is sometimes seen as synonymous with meditation. In this case, the term can cover not just a particular form of prayer, but a whole complex or sequence of actions, including the reading of Scripture and the use of set prayers, too.[15] In a much narrower sense, as Nicholls denounces it, mental prayer means mystical contemplation. This is God's gift alone, not achievable through any human effort. When François de Sales recommends mental prayer particularly, the way in which he phrases his advice allows a more general interpretation, in the sense of ordinary meditation, but it also allows a more specific reading, which refers to the involuntary experience of a mystical union:

> surtout je vous conseille la mentale et cordiale [oraison], et particulièrement celle qui se fait autour de la vie et Passion de Notre-Seigneur: en le regardant souvent par la meditation, toute votre âme se remplira de lui, vour apprendrez ses contenances, et formerez vos actions au modèle des siennes.[16]

The consequences of mental prayer, as can be seen, are far-reaching: it can lead to a perfect union with God, on the emotional and the intellectual level, and eventually to a fundamental change in one's daily life.

Some familiarity with the concept of mental prayer can be expected with an eighteenth-century devout audience. There are several manuals of instruction and commentary on mental prayer in English dating from the seventeenth and eighteenth centuries. Some of them are translations from the French or the Spanish, designed primarily for a recusant audience, as the authors were not only Catholics, but priests or even members of the Society of Jesus. Protestant readers may not have been familiar with these books at first hand. Some of them, however, went through several editions and some were printed in London. In the early seventeenth century the printer John Heigham (who also published an English translation of de Sales's *Introduction*) translated a Spanish treatise by Lewis of Puente, S.J., *Meditations upon the mysteries of our holie faith: with the practise of mental prayer touching the same*, which was printed by C. Boscard at St Omer in 1619. A Spanish treatise on mental prayer by Antonio de Molina was translated by John Sweetnam, S.J. under the title of *A treatise of mental prayer. In which is briefly declared the manner how to exercise the inward actes of vertues*, printed at the English College press in 1617. *The instruction of youth in Christian piety: taken out of the sacred Scriptures, and Holy Fathers; divided into five parts. With a very profitable instruction for meditation, or mental prayer*, was originally written in French by Charles Gobinet, Doctor of Divinity, of the House and Society of Sorbon, principal of the College of Plessis-Sorbon. Its English translation, based on the last French edition, was printed in London by Henry Hills, printer to the king, in 1687, and printed again, in a revised edition, with additional material, in London by F. Needham, in 1741. Henry Hills also published the *Introduction*.

In order to explore the wide spectrum of views on and definitions of mental prayer, it is helpful to look at some treatises more closely. *The method of mental prayer render'd practical and easie for all sorts of persons*, is a translation of *Methode facile d'oraison reduite en pratique* by R. F. Francis Nephew, S.J. and was printed by Thomas Hales in 1694. Francis Nephew explains in his preface that he wants to refute all prejudice against mental prayer, as being considered too hard to practice, not suitable to lay persons busy in the world, or requiring a very particular grace of God not given to everybody. He wants to help his readers to become masters of this 'Holy Art' by teaching them 'a short and easie manner how to Meditate [. . .] so that by one hours Reading, they may be sufficiently inform'd of the manner how to make their meditation well, and afterwards with very little pains may put their knowledge into practice' (A4).[17] Nephew defines mental prayer as 'serious reflections', naturally producing 'those good and pious desires, holy affections, and such sincere and efficacious resolutions, as reduce those good desires into practice, and move us to put in execution all our good designs'. It is not necessary to be very learned; on the contrary,

> The heart has a greater share in Prayer than the understanding; and there needs only a good heart, to render a Man capable of making a good prayer. The business is not to raise high thoughts, and quaint discourses; but to penetrate and be convinc'd of ordinary and plain truths. (p. 38)

Mental prayer, so Nephew explains, is nothing but 'the Exercise of the three faculties of our Soul, that is, of our Memory, Understanding, and Will', faculties that are used every day in 'any affair that concerns our Temporal interest, and our other Worldly business and employments' (p. 41). This sounds like 'ordinary' mental prayer, i.e. meditation exercises advertised for a comprehensive lay audience, which does not touch on anything remotely like a mystical union.

The *Catechism* by the Irish Catholic priest Andrew Donlevy, first published in Paris 1742 in a bilingual edition, with Gaelic and English on opposite pages, reprinted in English by the Catholic printer James Peter Coghlan in 1796, also insists on the necessity of mental prayer.[18] Donlevy calls meditation or mental prayer 'nothing else but a serious and frequent reflection upon the Truths of Salvation, to know them, to love them and to practice them'. He is convinced that mental prayer is a necessary part of devotion, not just for monks and nuns, but for ordinary people. He argues that its practice corresponds perfectly to what every conscientious artisan or merchant does to keep up his business, or the student in order to succeed with his subject: 'does he not think and re-think [...]? He applies his mind to comprehend it, to remember it, and to reap profit from what he learns.' So reflecting and thinking seriously upon salvation is one part of meditation. Another is affection: Donlevy deplores the saying of prayers by rote: in this case, the devotee's 'heart is silent and without motion'. But since it is 'the heart alone, that prays and obtains', one learns only from meditation 'to speak to God from the heart, and to hearken to him, when he speaks to our heart' (p. 286). Donlevy, like Nephew, insists on the affective aspect of mental prayer, but he also seems to give mystical union itself a wide berth.

Women also wrote on the subject. Lady Lucy Herbert's *Several Methods and Practices of Devotions appertaining to a Religious Life*, first printed in Bruges in 1743, recommends mental prayer. In § 10 she sums up its parts: preparation (consisting of 'presence of God, choice of matter, and invocation'), meditation proper (consisting of 'consideration, affection, and resolution'), and conclusion (consisting of 'thanksgiving, oblation, and petition'). In this, her outline conforms largely to de Sales's method. She describes prayer in general together with mental prayer, in § 2, 'Of the necessity of prayer, chiefly mental'. Of mental prayer in particular she says: 'As we are by our state obliged to tend to perfection, so consequently we are obliged to use mental prayer, and according to the progress we make therein, we may judge of that we make in perfection' (p. 4). While firmly holding, in § 3, that prayer in general is a gift of God, 'which is not acquired by human industry', but depending on God alone, and given only to those 'entirely abandoning themselves to his providence', she concedes that this gift entails 'a facility to raise our thoughts and unite our minds to God [...] by interior words, and sentiments produced from the heart' (p. 6). This allows of both interpretations of mental prayer: a general one, encompassing all forms of prayer that remain within the range of ordinary human comprehension, and a specific one that refers to mystical union: 'raise our thoughts and unite our minds to God'.

Application to prayer, however, being no guarantee for success, Lucy Herbert (in a manner very similar to de Sales) shows ways of dealing with distractions and dryness:

> We must not lose courage nor be dejected, when so dry that our understanding cannot discourse of any thing nor our will find any affection or gust, but in this case we ought now and then, to lift up our minds to God by short aspirations. (p. 7)

This dryness, however, is particularly painful to the devotee who has experienced a mystical union already and therefore suffers all the more from its prolonged absence. After a period of dryness the devotee should bring back her thoughts quietly to the subject of her meditation, and force herself to remain 'with respect and submission in the presence of God, kneeling humbly with your hands joyn'd, an[d] if you still wander from the subject, and are as dry as before, produce again some such aspirations, till your time allotted for prayer is ended' (p. 8). Patience and perseverance are essential. Lucy Herbert advises the devotee never to become discouraged, but to put herself again and again into God's presence, 'as if nothing had happen'd; and never to make reflexions upon what distracted us, netther [sic] by interior lamentations, or contrary acts, for that were to imprint them more in our mind'. This sounds like first-hand experience, advising the devotee to concentrate on the essential aim, not intensifying the negative state of mind by dwelling on it. Neither would it make sense to complain to God about a favour he has not granted, nor would it make sense to waste time crying over spilt milk. The author is well aware of the possibility of a mystical union as the highest aim and greatest gift awarded to constant prayer. But she counsels her readers not to seek this actively:

> [W]hatever degree of perfection we are arrived to, we must not of our selves presume higher than the common sort of prayer [. . .]: our study must be to labour courageously for solid virtue; and especialy [sic] the mortification of our Passions [. . .] As to a higher prayer,

God will raise us to it when he sees his time, and so much sooner, as we seek it less, and remain in the humble knowledge of our nothing, and unworthiness. (p. 9f.)

Humility is a key virtue, not just for keeping in mind the existential gap between God and humans, but also for remembering who gives and who receives. While the devotee continues to work on her self-improvement, this process is not supposed to lead to satisfaction with her achievement. Only if she gives herself over to God's will completely is there a chance of her receiving his presence.

Well aware of the painfulness of the time spent in the unsuccessful attempt to pray, Lucy Herbert draws a positive lesson from such apparent failure:

The securest mortifications and penances, according to the testimony of several holy, and experienced persons, is interior recollection and prayer; so that few or none, if they consulted nature, would not rather employ the like time in the most painful corporal labour, because that so the natural liberty of thinking is thereby constrain'd, our appetite suppress, our motions restrain'd, our will ty'd up, and our mind attentive not to give entrance to any thing that may distract or trouble the repose of our souls: in short the whole is indeed a constraint which is very painful. (p. 11)

In contrast to Francis Nephew's confidence that only 'very little pain' needs to be taken over prayer, Lucy Herbert explains that great pain, literally and figuratively, is the price to pay for successful devotion. The exchange of one's own volition for God's will is anything but easy, as the description of the complete enforced immobility demonstrates. The enormous willpower needed to achieve a state of mind that would allow a mystical union becomes very clear.

Richard Challoner, de Sales's translator, explains his concept of mental prayer in *Considerations upon Christian Truths and Christian Duties* (London, 1753). He defines it as a kind of prayer that

is not confined to any form of words, but is made in the secret closet of the heart; where the soul all alone, finds her God alone, and entertains herself with him. The advantages of this kind of prayer, beyond that which is only *vocal*, are, that it brings us nearer to God, and to

> his heavenly light; that it employs all the powers of the soul, viz. the memory, the understanding, and the will, about him; that it opens the eyes of the soul to the knowledge of God and of ourselves; and is the true school in which we learn to despise the world, and its cheating vanities; and to love God with our whole hearts. O my soul, see thou daily frequent this school of divine love! (p. 138)

This includes a mystical union: the eyes of the soul are open to the knowledge of God. The image of captivity corresponds to Lucy Herbert's. After having explained the method to be followed, Challoner explains that the prescribed steps of meditation can be suspended if God is willing to grant the soul the advance 'to the more perfect prayer of contemplation (in which she finds herself drawn nearer to god, quite alone with him, and absorpt in his love)'. In such circumstances, rules no longer apply: 'she must not be restrained, by any of these usual forms, or methods, from following that happy call; and thankfully yielding herself up a captive to divine love.' Challoner warns, however, of possible deception. Although the soul must 'follow God and his divine attractions', she must take recourse to the help of a guide, in order to avoid falling prey to 'suggestions of Satan, or of her own pride and self-love', which she may mistake for 'the motions of the Spirit of God' (p. 139). Challoner is well aware of the danger of false visions – his warning resonates with Nicholls's rejection of any aspiration to such a relationship of the soul with God. Catholic writers were well aware of the multiple difficulties posed by the claim to a mystical experience. Where they differ from a number of Protestant authors is in their belief in its possibility as well as its legitimacy.

Among those who turn against this aspect of mental prayer is John Owen, a Scottish Doctor of Divinity. He takes great pains to denounce above all Catholic forms of devotion as idolatrous and 'foolishly antick' (p. 19), but he is also wary of most set prayers, unless they stem from Scripture. In his preface to *A discourse of the work of the Holy Spirit in prayer. With a brief enquiry into the nature and use of mental prayer and forms* (Glasgow, 1757), he seems to argue firmly in favour of free, i.e. mental prayer: 'No persons, no churches [. . .] are obliged to confine themselves in their publick or private worship, onto set or humanely devised forms of prayer' (p. 27). He is convinced that all devotees are capable of praying by themselves, with the assistance of the Holy Ghost: 'nothing but the grace and the gifts of the Holy Ghost [. . .] is required in divine service, or can be admitted therein' (p. 21f.). However, in the discourse proper he goes to great lengths rejecting any kind of ineffable experience that might be the result of mental prayer. Whatever cannot be properly communicated to or even experienced by others falls under the verdict of a heated imagination, if not pretence and deceit:

> For no man can by the use of reason however advanced by spiritual light, understand such actings of the souls of other men or his own, as wherein there is no exercise of reason or understanding; such as these raptures are pretended to consist in [...] it had certainly been better for him to have kept his apprehensions of fancy to himself, than to express himself, in words which in their own proper sense are blasphemous, and whose best defensative [sic] is, that they are unintelligible [...] To allow such pretences is the ready way to introduce Babel into the church. (p 152f.)

Lack of certainty about these raptures must lead, Owen argues, to everlasting contention and dispute. On the other hand, Owen attempts to come to terms with the rational and emotional processes that are connected with prayer, searching for safe ground within the freedom opened up by the gifts of the Holy Ghost:

> That we allow of mental prayer and all actings of the mind in holy meditation, was before declared. Nor do we deny the usefulness or necessity of those other things of mortifying the affections and passions, of an entire resignation of the whole so[u]l unto God with complacency in him, so far as our nature is capable of them in this world. (p. 157)

The exercises of the mind that support prayer are acceptable to Owen, but the experience of the devotee in prayer is only condoned in so far as it is capable of being verbalized, and in so far as it can be shared in the community. Exceptional experiences like a mystical union are not to be trusted and should not be communicated.

But even though Protestant devotees might not have read any of those treatises, they could have been familiar with Henry Scougal's *The life of God in the soul of man: Or, The nature and excellency of the Christian religion*, which enjoyed an extensive reception throughout the eighteenth century in many different denominations. Scougal has only a comparatively small passage on mental prayer, but the divinity professor's book came, in different editions, with recommendatory prefaces by authorities from very different theological backgrounds, among them Bishop Burnet, William Wishart and John Wesley.[19] From its first printing in 1677, it went through multiple editions in Britain and America. Scougal explains that 'in prayer, we make the nearest approaches to God, and ly open to the influences of heaven: then it is that the Sun of righteousness doth visit us with his directest rays, and dissipateth our darkness, and imprinteth his image on our souls' (p. 101).

Comparing vocal prayer to mental prayer, Scougal calls the latter the 'more sublime kind of prayer' in which the soul 'takes a higher flight' and darts itself 'towards God in sighs and groans, and thoughts too big for expression' (p. 102). In mental prayer, the soul addresses itself to God 'in the profoundest adoration', or 'prostrates itself before him with the greatest confusion and sorrow, not daring to lift up its eyes, or utter one word in his presence', or it pants after God

> and sendeth up such vigorous and ardent desires, as no words can sufficiently express, continuing and repeating each of these acts as long as it finds itself upheld by the force and impulse of the previous meditation. This mental prayer is of all other the most effectual to purify the soul, and dispose it unto a holy and religious temper, and may be termed the great secret of devotion, and one of the most powerful instruments of the divine life.

Scougal does not want to replace other forms of prayer, which are more easily managed, because the time and effort required by mental prayer is so considerable that it overtaxes the devotee's capacity if attempted too often or for too long a period:

> every petition of this nature requireth so much time, and so great an intention of spirit [. . .]: to say nothing, that the deep sighs and heavings of the heart, which are wont to accompany it, are something oppressive to nature, and make it hard to continue long in them. But, certainly a few of these inward aspirations, will do more than a great many fluent and melting expressions. (p. 102f.)

Scougal takes prayer, and particularly mental prayer, for the proper exercise to '[mould] the soul into a holy frame' (p. 103). This is the linchpin of mental prayer: the devotee's aim is for the soul to resemble more and more the divine nature. At the same time, this is the problem for some theologians: human nature cannot – and should not – be so bold as to aspire to such proximity, as it cannot, in its fallen state, ever be worthy of such a relationship. Nor can humans achieve anything through their own efforts, as they are totally dependent on God's grace. Thus the underlying assumption of mental prayer, that some degree of mystical union is possible, would be considered heretical. Regarded from such a theological stance, the idea of, let alone the instructions for, mental prayer, would need to be deleted from any devotional manual.

V. Mental prayer in the *Introduction*

François de Sales did not invent prayer techniques. In his initial chapters on preparation, he refers explicitly to St Teresa of Avila for a method of learning to practise mental prayer. She proposes a fourfold process of preparation. First, you call to mind that God is present everywhere, including in your own heart; secondly, you place yourself in his presence. These are both acts of memory and will, but also acts of the imagination. The heart and the spirit are the focal places of this second step: God fills the heart and helps the spirit. In the third step the believer calls to mind that God sees and watches over all his children at all times. Finally, the believer is to imagine God in his human shape as one who is quite close, as one would imagine the circumstances and occupations of a good friend, and picture oneself with him. If one is in the presence of the Eucharist, however, it is not necessary to imagine God to be near, because he is really there.

We would not be surprised if Nicholls were to delete this last point, but he goes much further by cutting the whole of de Sales's chapter on preparation. Theologically, neither the omnipresence of God, nor the belief that God can see all of human kind is controversial. Visualizing scenes from the life of Christ is also not contrary to Protestant theology or devotional practice. But placing oneself in God's presence and imagining that one is close to him, as step two of the preparation advises, does not fit into the frame of mind that Nicholls considers appropriate for his Protestant readers. Also, since he has denounced the teaching of St Teresa of Avila particularly in his prefatory treatise, he cannot leave such extensive reference to her devotional method in his adaptation.

Both Dodwell and Nicholls delete all references to invocation of one's guardian angel, the Virgin Mary, or saints who were present at the particular event which serves as the focus of the meditation. François de Sales assumes that you can ask these witnesses to impart their 'sentiments et mouvements intérieurs' which they experienced, for example when they were present at the Passion of Christ, to you in your actual meditation. A gap of sixteen centuries and different languages as well as cultures could thus be overcome – mind could speak to mind, or rather heart to heart, as these communications seem to rely on wordless, intuitive exchanges. What de Sales asks for here is really an act of empathy that would rely primarily on the imagination, unless the emotions of these witnesses can be decoded on the basis of images of the Passion. It may be of interest in this context that the frontispiece used for the first three French editions depicted a pietà, which would lead the reader to two central concerns of the *Introduction*: meditation on the Passion of Christ, and veneration of the Virgin Mary. Opposition to imaginative acts of understanding, such as for example the empathetic reading of fiction takes for granted, is particularly strong in John Owen, who holds that we cannot understand anything we have not experienced ourselves.

When Nicholls polemicizes against the inspiration of the Holy Spirit in his treatise, he probably refers to a passage in his chapter VII (which would be chapter VIII in the source text and in Dodwell's adaptation), where he modifies his source considerably. The full passage appears in Dodwell. In certain situations, de Sales makes allowances for a departure from the prescribed stages of meditation. Here is Dodwell's version:

> For although ordinarily, Considerations ought to go before Affections and Resolutions: yet nevertheless, when the Holy Ghost poureth forth devout Affections, and holy Motions, into thy Soul, without discourse and consideration, thou must not then spend time in discoursing the points of thy exercise; for those discourses serve for no other end, but to stir up good Affections, which in this case, the Holy Ghost graciously stirreth up, and therefore need no discourse at all. In a word, whenever good affect, and devout motions offer themselves unto thee, receive them presently, and make them room in thy heart, whether they come before or after all the Considerations proposed in thy exercise. (p. 98f.)

And here is Nicholls's version:

> For although ordinarily consideration ought to go before affection and resolution, yet nevertheless, when the Holy Ghost giveth affections together with consideration, thou must not then seek consideration, since that serves for no other end but to stir up the affection. In a word, whensoever affections offer themselves, receive them, and make room for them, whether they come before or after consideration. (p. 65)

François de Sales assumes that after this preparation, the reader will feel in the presence of God and will pay homage to him accordingly, with great reverence, by invocation. He claims that the soul feels that she is – 'se sentant' – in the presence of God. Dodwell has the soul 'remembering and perceiving herself to be in the presence of God', but Nicholls has her only remember that she is there. Again, the sensual element is stronger in the Catholic source text than in the Protestant adaptations.

As a second step in the sequence of mental progress, the addressee can imagine the place where God is, on the basis of what they know from the Bible: often a scene from the Passion or the Crucifixion. The French author insists on the use of tangible topics that can be visualized at this point. If the readers are still beginners, learning how to pray, they should avoid abstract mysteries like the virtues, or the meaning of creation, as too complicated to keep their minds focused on. The imagination should remain firmly concentrated on the subject, picturing a scene helps to focus. Both Dodwell and Nicholls can agree with this.

This is followed by the chapter on considerations. It focuses on the understanding, as all three, de Sales, Dodwell and Nicholls, emphasize. De Sales's chapter heading refers only to the considerations, as does Nicholls's, while Dodwell adds 'and discourses of the understanding', thus emphasizing the labour of the mind necessary for this aspect of the exercise. However, these considerations are not purely intellectual, as was pointed out above.

The final steps of the meditation consist in the correct ending, and suitable transition back to the secular life. The effect of the meditation should be as long lasting as possible. One way of achieving this is the use of the nosegay. De Sales suggests, followed by both Dodwell and Nicholls, that the devotee should, in analogy to gathering a small bunch of flowers during a visit to a garden, 'gather a little Nose-gay of Devotion', consisting of 'one or two points which [we] have found most pleasing to our taste, and most agreeable to our understanding, upon which we might busie our mind, and [. . .] mentally smell thereon all the rest of the day'. The devotee should remain in her solitude while she does this, 'binding these points in our memory, as we would to flowers in a little Nose-gay' (Dodwell, p. 95). The vividly sensual image of the scent is tied to an occupation of the mind, which, it seems, makes it possible for both Dodwell and Nicholls to retain it.

Another passage, however, is stripped of its sensual overtones by Nicholls. While de Sales uses a vivid example to explain what his reader, Philotea, should do after she has prayed, transitioning to her daily occupations, Nicholls deletes this passage, adopting only the practical analogies: 'Accustom thy self to pass from Prayer to all kinds of Business, which thy Vocation and Profession, justly and lawfully requireth from thee [. . .], So let the Advocate learn to pass from Prayer to Pleading; the Merchant to his Traffick' (p. 64). Dodwell, however, follows de Sales's elaborate description of the imagined scene:

> At the end of thy exercise, take heed thou give not thy heart scope to range and wander: lest thou spill the delicious balm of good thoughts, and holy desires which thou hast received by prayer [. . .] endeavour to keep as long as is possible, the feeling and taste of those good effects, which thou hast received in meditation. Any Man that had received some precious liquor in a fair Porcellan, or *China Platter*, to carry home to his house, would go with it fair and softly, ever almost looking aside, but always either before him; for fear, that by stumbling, he should marr all, or else upon his vessel, to see that he spill not the liquor which he so much esteemeth: Even so must thou do when thou hast ended thy Meditation. (p. 96f.)

Thoughtfully, de Sales makes provision for occasions that do not go well and therefore will cause distress – the link between the devotee and God cannot always be established. Either the mind wanders, or no thought leads to a fruitful meditation. Several remedies can be tried: exclamations of short set prayers, reading passages from a devotional book, or performing external, physical acts of worship like lying on the ground (crossing one's arms or kissing a crucifix are deleted by Dodwell and Nicholls), provided one is in a private place, unobserved by anyone. If all this should fail, Philotea can take consolation in the knowledge that there are many visitors at court who never speak to the prince, or are noticed by him. Likewise, one can pay homage to God even when he does not seem to acknowledge it. Here, the patience advocated by Lucy Herbert springs to mind. She advised her reader simply to try again and again, until the time set aside for prayer has come to an end. Both adaptations describe the communion between God and Philotea as 'holy Inspirations, and interior Consolations' which are perceived as 'an inestimable honour' and 'a pleasure above all Pleasures'.[20] The terms used here do not seem to be so far away from a concept of mental prayer that would include the possibility of a mystical union, notwithstanding Nicholls's diatribe against 'mystical stuff' (p. 4 of the treatise *Of the Rise and Progress of the Spiritual Books in the Romish Church*). However, there appears to be a difference between a dialogic situation in which God and Philotea take part, and a total passive abandonment of the devotee to the presence of God in the soul, although both kinds of relationship are covered by the term mental prayer.

VI. Conclusion

Discussion of the method, function, form and effect of prayer in the Anglican Church takes place in shifting theological, political, and cultural contexts over historical periods with changing 'fashions'. This article can only focus on a snapshot, as it were, within a kaleidoscope of views held even at a single point in time. Generally speaking, Anglican theology contained statements on (mental) prayer that would have allowed the possibility of a beatific vision. Richard J. Ginn, in *The Politics of Prayer in Early Modern Britain*,[21] discusses the divine presence, inside and outside of churches, and the ways in which people could gain access to God in public worship, but also in private prayer. Ginn claims that the 'emphasis is always on the presence of God and the privilege of access [...] There was the implication of the view of worship as a mediated process leading to an unmediated access to the Divine' (p. 150). He quotes from John Moore, then Bishop of Norwich, *Of Religious Melancholy* (1692): 'Prayer will breed those ravishing, and glorious joys, because it brings us into a communion with the fountain of joy and glory. It opens heaven to us, gives us approach into the unaccessible glory' (p. 150). Such language is at least open to an interpretation which would not rule out a mystical union. Dodwell's adaptation of de Sales can be regarded as well within the boundaries of Anglican spirituality. Nicholls's defamatory attacks on supposedly (exclusively) Catholic heresies in his preface, although common at the time, seem not only unnecessary but also not completely in line with his main text. He eliminates the references to St Teresa of Avila as well as the chapter on preparation, but on the other hand much of the essence of de Sales's mental training in the *Introduction* survives in the adaptation.

Like other devotional manuals for a lay audience, the *Introduction* pursues the same aim on the micro and on the macro level, in the source text and in the adaptations: step-by-step, hourly, daily, lifelong training of the mind and the heart, towards the single goal of the love of God, from which will follow the love of man. The prescribed mental exercises are designed to train above all superb concentration and singleness of purpose, harnessing the will to a focus on specific images or ideas over a long stretch of time, eliminating desires and thoughts that do not fit into the truly devout frame of mind. They are also designed to train the imagination to picture scenes which will yield strong emotional, empathetic affects, participating in pain and misery, but also in joy and triumph. The self-discipline necessary to follow the rules of meditation earnestly and fervently will need constant practice. As this kind of prayer is coupled with frequent self-examination and confession, the devotee must have a most profound self-knowledge, not just relating to their shortcomings and sins, but also relating to their mental and emotional processes. Such an amount of introspection, and of verbal as well as emotional expression of mental life (the devotee does not only praise or plead with God – they are asked to tell him everything that moves them) seems to suggest that early modern and eighteenth-century Christians learnt to be very exceptional individuals, even though the manuals clearly describe ideal conditions.

It is not easy to determine what difference the various theological positions, resulting in the expurgated versions, may have made to the essence of the meditative training. While the basic mental training programme remained largely intact, the conceptions about the interaction between the soul and God on the deepest level of communication varied. This is demonstrated by the different positions on mental prayer in the sense of a mystical union. Behind this stand not only divergent theological, but also divergent anthropological concepts of human existence. There are also different degrees of emotional involvement and sensual experience envisioned in the adaptations. While the source text uses a full range of analogies relating to physical aspects of life, the adaptations – above all, Nicholls's text – are more restrained in this respect.

When we look at the material aids for devotion, be they body language, images or objects like a crucifix or a rosary, or even forms of the liturgy, the differences between source text and adaptations are greatest. While the Protestant rejection of a number of Catholic practices as idolatrous is mostly justified with reference to Scripture and early Christianity, there is more to this than an intellectual difference of opinion. We can only speculate on the effects of the interplay between the devotional training programme of the mental faculties on the one hand and the physical experience of different religio-cultural practices on the other hand. This is not a question of the 'better' religion, as Nicholls phrases it, but of the way in which such a transfer of a devotional manual works. In how far is the technical training programme still the same, when its whole framework, with its subsidiary reading, its liturgy, its physical expression of devotion, its sensual experience, and even its anthropological concept, is materially changed? Considering that mental processes never take place without a firm anchoring in a body, in space and time, and in the individual's cultural practice, and social as well as textual community, we must assume that devotion, in crossing denominational and linguistic boundaries, in this case at least, undergoes significant changes.

Notes

[1] The 1619 edition is also considered definitive by modern scholarship: André Ravier (ed.), *Saint François de Sales. Oeuvres* (Paris, 1969).

[2] Helen C. White, *The Tudor Books of Private Devotion* (Madison, WI, 1951), p. 170: 'Even when the lines between Catholic and Protestant had been clearly drawn, and the controversial battle joined on scores and issues, English devotional writers still went on translating and adapting Continental works of devotion from Catholic as well as Protestant sources.'

[3] Sabine Volk-Birke, 'Catholic devotion fitted for the use of Protestants. François de Sales' *Introduction à Vie Dévote* in France and Britain', in a special edition of *JECS*, 2018 (accepted).

[4] H. Dodwell, *An Introduction to a Devout Life containing especially, a prudent method for spiritual closet-exercises, and remedies against the difficulties ordinarily occurring in the conduct of a pious life, Fitted for the use of Protestants, by Henry Dodwell* (Dublin, 1673), sig. f5.

[5] Ravier (ed.), *Saint François de Sales. Oeuvres*, pp. 19–317, p. 29.

[6] From the third edition, part three is reserved for learning how to cultivate virtue, part four deals with ordinary temptations, and part five teaches how to renew the soul and persevere in the devotional life. The editor André Ravier regards the third edition as authoritative; Bishop Challoner also uses the third edition as source text for his English translation in 1762.

[7] William Nicholls, *François de Sales, An introduction to a devout life, by Francis Sales, Bishop and Prince of Geneva. Translated and reformed from the Errors of the Popish Edition. To which is perfixed* [sic] *a Discourse, of the Rise and Progress of the Spiritual Books in the*

Romish Church by William Nicholls D. D. (London, 1701). The *Discourse* does not have printed page numbers. The references given here rely on the pencilled page numbers in the copy in the British Library that I consulted. Their numbers are independent of the printed pagination of the *Introduction*.

8 De Sales refers only to the considerations in his chapter heading, as does Nicholls, while Dodwell adds 'and discourses of the understanding'.

9 Nicholls exchanges Dodwell's term 'taste' for 'satisfaction', thus playing down – as he does elsewhere – the sensual aspect of the prayer experience.

10 '[S]i est-ce que le Saint-Esprit vous donnant les affections avant la consideration, vous ne devez pas rechercher la consideration, puisqu'elle ne se fait que pour émouvoir l'affection.'

11 Although Alec Ryrie discusses many aspects of prayer in *Being Protestant in Reformation Britain* (Oxford, 2013), he does not explicitly address the issue of mental prayer in the sense of spiritual union with God. He deals with the related concepts of desire, wordless prayer, the emotional component of Protestant prayer, the return to Passion piety and other features of devotion which preserved or revived medieval traditions in early modern Britain, but he steers clear of the knotty problem of how closely the soul can really approach God in prayer, and how much of the beatific vision is permitted on earth.

12 'It is easy also to understand that Meditation, and mental Prayer, and daily Examination, are the best Exercises for this purpose [i.e. overcoming practical prejudices]; and that not only in public, whether in Churches or Families, but especially such as are private and particular' (a4).

13 When Nicholls polemicizes against the inspiration of the Holy Spirit in his treatise, he probably refers to a passage in his chapter VII, where he modifies his source considerably, but we find the full passage in Dodwell's adaptation in chapter VIII. In certain situations, de Sales makes allowances for a departure from the prescribed stages of meditation.

14 In the relevant chapters in part II, however, Nicholls has not deleted all references to mental prayer. Its general recommendation in chapter I may have slipped his attention: 'But moreover I recommend to thee, mental and cordial Prayer, and especially that which hath for its subject, the Life and Passion of our Lord, for beholding him often by meditation, thy Soul will be filled with him, thou wilt learn his carriage, and frame thy actions according to the model of his. [. . .] Employ in it every day an hour before Dinner.' In the following chapters he has removed long passages, above all those dealing with the four steps of preparation as recommended by St Teresa of Avila.

15 See Alec Ryrie, *Being Protestant in Reformation Britain* (Oxford, 2013), on the wide range of meanings of meditation in early modern Britain, pp. 108–18.

16 François de Sales, *Introduction*, part II, ch. 1, in Ravier (ed.), *Saint François de Sales. Oeuvres*, p. 79.

17 White, in *The Tudor Books of Private Devotion*, draws attention to the gap in the experience and training between the professional and the layman: 'The magnitude of the undertaking of a systematic and extended program of prayer for the layman who was not trained for it was not easy for the professional to grasp. It is never easy for the man who has a special aptitude for a certain way of life, and who has trained himself systematically in its techniques, to remember afterwards what that field looked like to him before he achieved his mastery, and still less easy is it for him to envisage the nature of the problems it offers to the man who not only has not enjoyed his opportunities for training but has neither his impelling interest in nor his talent for the pursuit at the center of his own life' (p. 153).

18 Andrew Donlevy, *The catechism, or Christian doctrine, by way of question and answer; drawn from the express word of God, and other pure sources* (London, 1796).

[19] See the seminal article on the reception of Scougal by Isabel Rivers, 'Scougal's *The Life of God in the Soul of Man*. The fortunes of a book 1676–1830', in Ruth Savage (ed.), *Philosophy and Religion in Enlightenment Britain: New Case Studies* (Oxford, 2012), pp. 1–45: 'the study of its fortunes can show us how, for a period of over a hundred and fifty years, editors and readers from different denominations and of a variety of intellectual and religious leanings were able to shape the meaning of the work to suit their own needs' (p. 2). The book had 'an extremely wide distribution through two separate and unrelated channels, one moderate Scottish Presbyterian and the other English Methodist, existing alongside the successive London editions deriving from Burnet and Cockburn' (p. 16).

[20] Dodwell, *An Introduction to a Devout Life ... Fitted for the use of Protestants*, p. 110; Nicholls, *François de Sales, An introduction to a devout life*, p. 67.

[21] Richard J. Ginn, *The Politics of Prayer in Early Modern Britain. Church and State in Seventeenth-century England* (London, New York, 2007).

INDEX

A

Abenaki, people, 56
Allin, James, 15, 16
America, 3, 4, 6, 102
Ambrose, Isaac, 16–18
Amsterdam, 72
Anderson, John, 95
Anglicanism, *see* Church of England
Anti-Catholicism, 91–2, 104
Appleton, Nathaniel, 103
Arndt, Johann, 96
atheism, 96
Augustine, 104
Augustus III, King of Saxony, 38
Ave Maria, *see* Hail Mary
Avila, St Teresa of, 9, 113, 122, 127
Aztecs, 2

B

Baptists, 95
Barclay, Robert, 103
Barrow, Isaac, 104
Battle of Quebec, 91
Baxter, Richard, 17
Bayly, Lewis, 16
Beauty of Holiness in the Common Prayer, 95
Beccaria, Cesare, 36, 51
Benedictus, 95, 98
Bolontov, Andrei, 47–8
Book of Common Prayer, 95, 96, 103
books of prayers, 4, 5

Boston, Massachusetts, 12, 15, 83, 86
Bradstreet, Anne, 13, 18–20
branding, 44–5
Britain, 3, 102, 103
Brooks, Thomas, 81
Bull, George, Bishop, 105
Burnham, Michelle, 20

C

Cambridge, Massachusetts, 12
Canada, 58, 61, 66
captivity, 56–67, 12–32
captivity narratives, 57, 66, 12–32
Carroll, Lorrayne, 13
catechism, 97, 98, 116
Catherine II, Empress of Russia, 36, 40, 47
Challoner, Bishop Richard, 108, 118–19
Chambly, Quebec, 58
Chauncey, Charles, 81
Chinese Rites Controversy, 2
Christian's Memorandum-Book; or, Family Instructor, 97
Church of England, 4, 5, 8, 82, 95, 96, 102, 103, 109, 110, 111, 126, 128
Church of Scotland, 95
Clark, Roger, 96
Club, in a Dialogue between Father and Son, 103
Clutterbuck, John, 97
Coghlan, James Peter, 116

Index

Colman, Benjamin, 83, 86, 87, 103
colonies, 2
Colwall, Daniel, 81
Columbus, Christopher, 1
Commentary on the Book of Common Prayer, 110
Conformists, 95
Congregationalism, 103
Considerations upon Christian Truths and Christian Duties, 118–19
Cortez, Hernan, 2
creation of place, 111, 124

D
Dane, John, 18–20
Daniel, 32
David, King, 22–6, 32
Deborah, 94
death sentence, 7, 36–52
death-bed spiritual memoirs, 19
Deerfield Raid, 7, 56–67
Defoe, Daniel, 73–5, 77–8, 81, 82, 83
Deism, 97
De La Chatardie, Marquis, 37
DeLaune, Thomas, 95
De Maistre, Joseph, 36
de Sales, Francis, 8, 109–14, 122–8
Derounian-Stodola, Zabelle, 20, 26
Diebold, Robert K., 20, 28
Discourse of the work of the Holy Spirit in prayer, 119–20
Dissenters, 95, 96
Dodwell, Henry, 109–13, 123–8
Donlevy, Andrew, 116
Donskoi monastery, 38, 39
Douay catechism, 98
Downing, David, 20
Drummond, Thomas, 100
drunkenness, 30
Dryden, John, 77

Dunton, John, 83
Dustan, Hannah, 32

E
East India Company, 82
ejaculatory prayer, 59–61
Elizabeth, 93–4, 96, 99
Elizabeth, Empress of Russia, 6, 7, 36–52
Elphinson, James, *A Collection of Poems*, 100–1
England, 56
Enlightenment, 96, 97, 104, 105
Eucharist, 4
Evelyn, John, 73, 74

F
Finland, 43
First Church of Boston, 15
Fisk, Joseph, 91–2
Foxe, John, 96
France, 3, 56, 84–5
funeral sermons, 102, 103
funerals, 8, 70–88

G
Gerrish, Martha, 103
Glorious Revolution, 93
Goodhue, Sarah, 18–20
'Great Awakening', 104
Green, Samuel, 12, 19
Gyllenborg, Carl, 43

H
Hail Mary, 93–4, 112
Hambrick-Stowe, Charles, 17–18, 59
Hannah, 32, 94

Hanover, House of, 93
Harvard University, 15
Henwood, Dawn, 20–1, 26
Herbert, Lady Lucy, 116–18, 126
High Church, 96, 97
Hill, Edmund, 85–6
Hill, Joseph, 81
History of the Incarnation, Life, Doctrine, and Miracles, 101
Hoar, Leonard, 15
Holmes, Robert, 102
Hubbard, William, 12–13, 23
Huron, 56
hymns, 97

I
idolatry, 91, 92, 95
Iaguzhinskii, Pavel, 52
Ignatius of Loyola, 94
Immaculate Conception, 92
intercessory prayers, 61–3
Introduction to a Devout Life, 109, 110, 113, 123–8
Iroquois of the Mountain, 56

J
Jael, 32
James II, 93
Jesuits, 63
Job, 24–5
Jonathan, 22
Joseph, 32

K
Kahanwake, 56, 63
Kiev, 39
King Philip's War (also Metacom's War), 12, 27–9, 56

L
Latitudinarian, 103
Leontyev, M. I., 40
Lestocq, Johann, 37
Life of God in the Soul of Man, 120–2
London, 13, 27, 80–1, 82
Longmeadow, Massachusetts, 59, 61, 63, 65, 67
lotteries, 81–2
Low Church, 102, 103
Luther, Martin, 94, 96, 98, 103
Lynch, Kathleen, 19–20

M
Mack, Phyllis, 100
Magnificat, 91–105
Mary II, Queen of England, 82
Massachusetts, 2, 7
Mather, Cotton, 18, 32, 103
Mather, Increase, 6, 13, 16, 22, 26, 30, 31, 32 92
Mather, Maria, 16
meditation, 4
merchants, 70–88
Metacom's War, *see* King Phillip's War
Method of mental prayer render'd practical and easie for all sort of persons, 115
Methodism, 100, 104
Middlesex County, 28
millennialism, 96
Mexico, 3
Mohawks, 56, 61
Monoco (Nipmuc sachem), 27–9
Montreal, 63
morning prayer, 4
Moscow, 42
Mourning War, 56
mystical union, 9, 113, 114, 116, 117, 118, 119, 120, 126

133

N

Narragansett, 2
narrative prayer, 63–4
Native Americans, 2, 3, 6, 7, 12, 20, 24, 26, 27, 28, 29, 30; *see also* references to specific peoples
Nephew, R. F. Francis, S. J., 115, 116, 118
Neuman, Meredith, 15
New England, 2, 3, 12, 15, 27, 56, 57, 58, 61, 65, 92, 103
New France, 56, 57
Nicholls, William, 109, 110–14, 122–8
Nipmuc, 2, 27
nosegay, 108, 124–5
Nunc Dimittis, 95, 98

O

Oakes, Urian, 22–3
Okes, Nicholas, 109, 110
Oldham, John, 94
Ostermann, A. I., 42
Our Father, prayer, 8, 112
Owen, John, 119–20, 123

P

parliament, 93
Pennacooks, 56, 57
Pennsylvania, 3
Pentecostalism, 3
Peter the Great, Emperor of Russia, 38, 41, 46, 48
Peters, Christine, 93, 94
Philadelphian Society, 96
Pocumtuck, 56
Popery, 111
Popish Plot, 94
posture, 4, 110
prayer, mental, 108, 109, 113–28

preparatory prayer, 65–7
Presbyterianism, 95, 103
Principles of the Christian Religion Explained, 92–3
Protestantism, 5, 6, 8, 9, 71, 72, 91–105
Providence, 57
Pugachev's Rebellion, 36
Puritans, 2, 12–32, 103

Q

Quakers, 103
Queen Anne's War, *see* War of Spanish Succession
Quinnapin, sachem, 29–30

R

Ragervik, 46–8, 51
rape, 27–30
Rise and Progress of the Spiritual Books in the Romish Church, 111, 126
Roach, Richard, 96
Rogers, Timothy, 83, 84, 85, 102
Roman Catholicism, 2, 5, 6, 8, 61, 98, 99, 102, 104, 105, 109, 110, 111, 114, 119, 126, 128
rosary, 8, 94, 110, 128
Rowlandson, Joseph, 14, 15, 31
Rowlandson, Mary, 6, 7, 12–32
Royal Society, 75–6, 81
Russia, 3, 6, 7, 36–52
Russo-Swedish war, 43
Ryder, Joseph, 76

S

Salisbury, Neal, 28
Saltonstall, Nathaniel, 13, 27–9
Saul, King, 22
Schwartz, Jacob, 37

Scougal, Henry, 120–2
Scudder, Henry, 18
Several Methods and Practices of Devotions appertaining to a Religious Life, 116–18
Shafirov, P.P., 41–2
Shcherbatov, Prince Mikhail, 36, 37, 50
Shepard, Thomas, *The Sincere Convert*, 15
Shuvalov, P. I., 49
Society of Friends, *see* Quakers
Solomon, King, 73, 74
Solovyov, S. M., 52
spiritual autobiographies, 17–20
Sprat, Thomas, 74
state prayers, 4
Stillingfleet, Edward, 102
Stoddard, David, 86–7
St Petersburg, 41
Sudakov, Ivan, 39
Swansea, Massachusetts, 28

T
Mary Talcott, *see* Mary Rowlandson
Talcott, Samuel, 31
Te Deum, 95
Tenochtitlan, 2
Thacher, Thomas, 31
Thomas, Sir Dalby, 81
Tillotson, John, 102, 103, 104
Toulouse, Teresa, 13
Trauma, 26, 58
Turberville, Henry, 98

U
Usher, Bridget Hoar, 15
Usher, Hezekiah, Jr., 15

V
Venite, 95
Vespucci, Amerigo, 1
Virgin Mary, 5, 8, 91–105, 110, 122
Vorontsov, M. I., 37, 49
Vyborg, 37

W
Walker, Nathaniel, 83, 84
Wampanoag, 2
War of Spanish Succession (Queen Anne's War), 56
Warner, Ferdinando, 102
Watts, Isaac, 98–9
Weber, Max, 70–1
Weetamoo, sachem, 29
Wesley, John, 99–100, 101
West, Benjamin, 91
Wheatly, Charles, 97
Whore of Babylon, 92
Williams, Esther, 57
Williams, Eunice, 57, 61–3
Williams, Eunice Mather, 56, 57, 58
Williams, Jerusha, 57
Williams, John (father), 56
Williams, John (son), 57
Williams, Samuel, 57
Williams, Stephen, 7, 8, 56–69
Williams, Warham, 57, 58
witchcraft, 49
women, 5
women's authorship, 12–14
Woodbridge, Benjamin, 31

ISBN   978-1-78683-225-2
eISBN   978-1-78683-226-9
ISSN (Print)   2057-4517
ISSN (Online)   2057-4525

The Journal of Religious History, Literature and Culture
© University of Wales, 2017
Articles and reviews © The Contributors, 2017

Reprinted 2018

Contributors to *The Journal of Religious History, Literature and Culture* should refer enquiries to the journal page at www.uwp.co.uk or e-mail press@press.wales. ac.uk requesting notes for contributors.

Advertising enquiries should be sent to the Sales and Marketing Department at the University of Wales Press, at the address below.

Subscriptions: *The Journal of Religious History, Literature and Culture* is published twice a year in June and October. The annual subscription for institutions is
£95 (print only), £85 (online only) or £140 (combined); and for individuals is £25 (print or online only) or £40 (combined). Subscription orders should be sent to University of Wales Press, 10 Columbus Walk, Brigantine Place, Cardiff, CF10 4UP. Tel: (029) 2049 6899; e-mail: press@press.wales.ac.uk.